SEAN WEAFER

The Highly Trusted Advisor

How To Lead Teams And Win Clients In
The Hybrid Age

○ SEANWEAFER.COM

For my amazing and beautiful family, Sharon, Nicholas, Gregory and Kai (our dog!).

For my Mom, Eileen and my Dad, Peter, for all that you have given me.

To my mentor, Dr. Denis Waitley, for your guidance and friendship.

Contents

Preface

Are you in a leadership or management role and a little challenged when it comes to successfully engaging and influencing key internal stakeholders, your team or maybe with projecting your leadership presence and profile within the wider firm especially in a more remote and hybrid world?

Are you a professional in practice, sales executive or entrepreneur who is technically excellent at what you do but who sometimes struggle to maintain your position of trust, access and influence in a digital and hybrid world where clients have so much more choice?

Or are you an executive or 'internal' advisor such as a HR team, an IT, Finance, Operations or Inside Sales team who would benefit from projecting your value to other parts of the organisation or to key stakeholders, influencers and 'internal' clients through networking, presenting and engaging?

If so, then this book is for you.

In an increasingly flat-lined, matrix-managed and hybrid world it's not enough just to be an expert at our role anymore, we must also be compelling influencers and communicators.

It's not enough to continue to lead with traditional reflexive Masculine values of expertise, logic, competition and command and control, we must now also deploy powerful reflective Feminine values such as collaboration, synergy, nurture and empathy.

In a world where AI (artificial intelligence) is replacing traditional expertise and the management and running of the transactional aspects of business and where leadership and selling have increasingly become more online and remote, then the ability of skilled human influencers to provide empathy, encouragement and care to lead, to advise and to inspire will become the sought-after skillset.

Modern leadership and sales professionals now have to excel at the practical application of relationship intelligence skills and must be able to build compelling and highly trusted client and stakeholder relationships on a one-to-one or on a one-to-many level.

Today leadership and sales are just two sides of the same coin, that of being of service to others. Leaders must now serve their 'internal clients' (colleagues, team members and senior stakeholders) to drive performance, recognition and value. Sales professionals must serve their external clients to drive perceived value and revenue.

It is only through mastering the ability to be more influential, more successful at connecting, engaging and persuading others (whether they are colleagues or clients) in this new hybrid world that a leader, executive or sales professional can strengthen and deepen their bond and their value to their firms and their clients.

This book shows how to do this successfully in very practical ways so that you create new levels of trust, influence and engagement with colleagues, clients and key stakeholders and boost your professional and personal value both online and offline.

It explores how to use proven, practical tools of EQ (emotional or relationship intelligence) so that we can successfully deploy our IQ (technical intelligence) to project brand value, executive presence and leadership influence to key people in our organisation OR to win and retain high value clients.

In effect, it shows us how to move from simply being expert executives and professionals to becoming highly trusted and valued advisors that can get things done with little or no resistance to our messages, proposals or suggestions.

In 'The Highly Trusted Advisor: How to Lead Teams and Win Clients in a Hybrid World' (and the products and coaching programs that support the book) I've distilled what the world's greatest leaders, sales influencers, coaches and professionals do naturally into a proven set of techniques and tools to influence key stakeholders to lead successful teams and win high value clients in today's hybrid world of artificial intelligence, remote working and live engagement.

In today's hybrid world:

Share of Influence = Share of Quality Attention

Getting access and the attention of valuable stakeholders and clients in today's world has become more challenging and standing out from the crowd even more challenging, as the level of distraction and competition for their attention increases every day.

In this book I share thirty years and more of experience in how to create compelling business messages, in how to access people through personal contact (and now online) networking, how to build high levels of trust and influence and a strong personal brand, project executive presence, key client and stakeholder meeting management skills and master presentation and pitching skills, even how to manage your professional time and sharpen your focus.

This book takes you step-by-step through the skills necessary to help you to create and nurture your colleagues, your stakeholders and your clients so that you are recognised as a valued highly trusted business leader, sales advisor and professional in your business or can win and retain long-term, repeatable profitable income streams for your business in a hybrid world.

Sean Weafer.
Dublin, February 2021

1

Trust is No Longer Enough

Today it is no longer enough just to be trusted by a colleague, a stakeholder or a client. Now we have to be able to create a 'High Trust' relationship. However, what exactly do I mean by 'High Trust'? To explain, let me ask if you've ever noticed that there are 'degrees of trust' in your personal and professional relationships?

For example, do you have business relationships with people that you may trust and may even like, but you still don't share everything with them?

At the same time don't we *also* have relationships with people with whom we have a high degree of trust and with whom we happily share *everything*. Relationships where we have *absolutely* no reservation or hesitation whatsoever in sharing everything because we see them as our 'go to' person if we ever have a problem that needs solving. We usually call *them* before we call anyone else.

This is what I call a 'high trust' relationship and it is the level of trust that we need to reach with others if we want to become compelling advisors, leaders, professionals, coaches, business developers and sales professionals in the workplace, so that we can create cultures of trust and transparency in our organisations or create long-term profitable client relationships.

In today's ever-changing workplace the ability to create relationships with colleagues and clients that they find *compelling and engaging* and that encourages them to share all of their concerns, wants and needs with us (seeing us as valuable partners in their business or their career), can create limitless opportunities for us.

If we become the 'go to' person for them, if we become the first person they think of when it comes to calling for help then that gives us a highly trusted position of access, influence and value with them.

In addition, in this new online and offline world business values are changing rapidly.

In the past business values were strongly Masculine. They were about competition, dominance, hierarchy, profit, position, authority, expertise, skills, logic and who had the power. In most situations one's authority, position, status and influence came from our technical skills or professional expertise, your IQ or TQ (Technical intelligence Quotient).

These were the values of the *Masculine Age*. The values of this age moved us from simple hunter-gatherers and inspired us to build cities, to explore our world, to create societies and invent the technology to extend our physiology and psychology into space and powers our lives today. That age however is passing away.

Today the values that are evolving in business, in leadership, sales and in wider society are the values of the Feminine Age. It is no longer about status and control that is not derived from simple technical expertise but 'power through and with people'.

Values such as co-operation, collaboration, connection and community, compassion, service, emotion, intuition, innovation, creativity and nurture are slowly replacing and rebalancing many of the old Masculine values as we move into a world that is enabled by communications and AI technology.

Modern leadership is about recognising, respecting and balancing all of these values and energies in a leader. Increasingly, leadership is genderless.

With colleagues and with clients you may already find that they *want* to feel more engaged in the creation of their own solutions, they *want* to be a part of the process more than ever before.

They want greater involvement in the process of co-creating solutions and sharing more of the ownership around outcomes rather than simply being directed or led into pre-determined outcomes that we, as the 'experts', have decided.

Today clients and colleagues want 'rapporteurs' (advisors and leaders who can build trusted relationships, advise and serve) and not 'reporters' (people who simply tell them what they should do or simply bring information to them without making it meaningful).

They increasingly want advisors and partners, people who lead and sell through influence and collaboration, that they can engage and connect with. Executives who focus on nurturing, advising and shaping the very best of solutions for their colleague's or client's business needs.

Authority and influence are now accomplished through the size, strength and depth of your networks and your ability to build high levels of trust, minimise resistance and powerfully influence and coach the people in those networks rather than just your technical expertise or position.

The robots and AI are already here and impacting on professions, service and manufacturing companies alike. But they are unlikely to replace skilled human influencers, at least not in the short term. We may not have the advantage in logical processing and reasoning anymore but we do have the emotional factor and that stimulates emotion, trust, loyalty creativity and innovation in others. That remains our edge and a Highly Trusted Advisor knows how to draw from and successfully balance both expertise and influence.

2

IQ v EQ

In the past many executives and professionals relied solely on their (or others) technical expertise, their IQ or 'intelligence quotient', to deliver value to colleagues or clients. It was enough to be an expert or specialist, to arrive, to get the job done and then leave.

But now people expect a leader or professional to have a high EQ (Emotional intelligence Quotient), able to create a compelling and engaged relationship and demonstrate a real understanding of their concerns and fears and all of this *before* they allow you to deploy or use your IQ or technical knowledge.

Today it is our ability to first deploy our EQ (or trust and influence) that ensures that we get the chance to deploy our IQ or expertise and skills. Today's professionals are required to have a significantly greater degree of understanding of the emotional dynamics that impact on relationships and the most important of these is trust.

Trust is a powerful thing for nothing happens and nobody acts without first having achieved some form of trust in a person or an undertaking.

No directions are carried out and no purchase orders are placed without trust.

Trust is essential to business. What happens when trust is broken is that things spiral down to a stop and we face recession. Banks don't lend, businesses don't invest, jobs become insecure and customers don't spend. Trust is a function of rapport and 'High Trust' (and thus strong connection and influence) is a function of deep rapport.

Trust comes where there is a recognition and acceptance of our mutual shared experience or need and where we have moved a relationship (be it with a client or a key stakeholder within our own business) beyond simply communicating with a person to where we connect, influence and engage with them on a personal and compelling level.

Where there is trust there is acceptance and where there is acceptance a person is open to being positively and ethically influenced and only then can change happen and decisions be made.

'High' trust in business comes not from corporate communications or from big advertising campaigns but from the work of the individual leader or professional who builds it, one person at a time, colleague by colleague, client by client.

Good business has always been *relational* or focused on people. Where engaging with the client or a colleague becomes not about the product or the service or the project but about the *experience* that a person gets from having engaged with us. Not just what they *think* but what they *feel*.

Growing our trust and influence depends on the quality of our relationships and this is an emotional art. Knowing how to manage a person's *emotional* responses is the key to winning their support and collaboration or business or buying decisions.

Great business development and leadership is about the psychological and emotional dynamics of relationships, how well we can apply our 'emotional quotient' to leadership and ethical selling and a key part of that is first creating a highly trusted relationship.

The key to business success is therefore about learning how to create compelling, collaborative and co-creative staff and client relationships by creating and nurturing a high degree of trust between us and other people.

After the market upheavals of the first decade of the century the constant need to continue to rebuild trust in business, even today, means that we have to continually re-define our views and even our language about other people. We have to start walking in the other person's shoes, to see things from their perspective and seek to understand the values that drive their needs and thus their decisions.

What made it even more challenging was that the global Covid19 pandemic forced much of this activity online to where we now have to operate in a two-dimensional rather than a three-dimensional environment, online as opposed to previously live and 'in-person' environments, or now a fusion of the two, our new 'hybrid' world.

Another element that is fundamental to the idea of a 'High Trust' relationship and that heightens a person's experience of us, is how closely we align the values of what we are offering to the values of the key stakeholder, colleague or client.

Values are global and abstract things for example, security, power, money, control, time and even harmony can all be defined as values. They can't really be explained or broken down any further, they are what they are and they each have a unique prioritisation, resonance and meaning with each person.

However, people do not share their values easily and sometimes are even unsure of what those values are. By creating powerful rapport and high trust with a person, by having them willingly accept us and our connection with them and then guiding them through a series of questions, we can rapidly identify and prioritise their key buying and decision-making values.

By aligning another person's unique values with the values of what *we* want that person's support for, we can create a resistance-free relationship where we become highly trusted influencers and valued colleagues and business partners.

The future of business is in the hands of well-trained highly trusted advisors, leaders and coaches. We grow business profits and team and board performance by being ethical, relational and focused on creating a unique experience for the other people that we serve.

People no longer need their leaders or sales advisors to be the experts, information providers, directors or 'brochure carriers' of the past because they have a much faster, mobile and responsive means of getting information, the mobile 'always on' Internet (or corporate Intranet).

Now people really need us *to interpret* the information that they have already gathered, to *advise* them on making the very best decisions.

They want us to understand where they are, to coach them on the best way forward, to help solve their problems, to help them grow and succeed and to walk the journey with them.

What people need now are advisors who can *interpret the information* in a way that is meaningful and of value to them. They require not just a product, a service or direction but *a collaborative experience* and we must learn to create that experience from the moment that we meet with them.

As an executive in a leadership role our job is now more about 'creating the environment in which our people can excel' and to do this we need to be more collaborative, inclusive and well versed in the skills of influence. In addition, we need to be more capable of building a strong personal brand and projecting executive presence in order to have more leadership influence.

As sales professionals our job is to help create relationships where our clients will thank us for identifying and providing a solution to one (or more) of the 4 Principles of Value in Selling; 1. Save Me Time 2. Save Me Money 3. Solve My Problems and 4. Make Me Feel Good

Highly trusted executives and professionals ensure they are well versed in the relationship arts of influence, persuasion and psychology and actively use technology and social platforms to leverage their brand and their engagement in support of their clients and colleagues.

3

Points of Compelling Relevance

This chapter has a particular focus on what it takes to be a highly trusted advisor in a business development or sales position but carries lessons for us all on how to first engage, then compel another persons' attention.

To be truly influential and valued, relationships need to be *relational* or focused on people. Where client and team relationships become what they should be, not about the product or the project or the expertise but about the *experience* that the other person gets through engaging with us.

That experience starts with 'first contact' or the moment that we get in front of an important prospect, client, colleague or stakeholder (and even long before that, in the form of the messages on our literature or website or our LinkedIn profile) when their decisions about us, our value to them, our products or our services, are first beginning to form.

For most people 'first contact' is much more powerful when it is in person rather than over the phone or on an online meeting app. A contact made when one has networked to meet another person as opposed to simply 'cold calling' them is significantly more user friendly and open to engagement. However, today we need to be versed in both the online and offline psychology of engagement.

An executive or professional who wishes to become a highly trusted advisor must first understand that any and all barriers that come between us and the other person first need to be minimised before we can build high levels of trust or influence.

In addition, he or she understands the dollar, euro or pound value of an hour attempting to build relationships online with people they have not yet met. As a result, they prefer to do in-person 'hot coffees' not 'cold calls'.

For professional and executives who want to be influential business developers and advisors it's useful to remember that business development (and especially 'selling') has for decades been viewed as the poor and low-status end of business.

Professional 'selling' has always been what I call a mainly 'accidental' profession, as people tended to 'fall into it' as they progressed in their career rather than people actually choosing to grow up to be a 'salesperson'.

I say 'professional selling' in the sense of a specific sales or business development role. Leaders and managers are also constantly selling, e.g., trying to get agreement from stakeholders, pitching for more budget and resources, getting support for proposals, winning trust with their teams.

Today, *everybody sells* (either to external prospects or to internal decision makers and colleagues) as leaders we sell to internal clients just as much as sales professionals and business developers sell to external clients.

It's useful to be reminded of the origin of the word 'selling'. It is said it evolved from a root word meaning *'to be of service'*. But over the years it has developed into a stereotypical image of being a high pressure, 'hard' and a distinctly unpleasant experience for the person on the receiving end.

I think we should refocus on being of service in both sales and in leadership today. In fact, the term 'servant leadership' has been in fashion for some time now, implying that leadership comes from the ability to be of service to one's team and creating the environment in which the individual team members can personally excel, hence why professional coaching skills are such a 'must-have' for leaders in today's hybrid world.

We should remember that while we are obviously in the business of being 'of service' to our clients or customers (for that's how we drive profits) as leaders we are also in the business of being of service to our team members and colleagues.

In today's world of 'mass distraction' being able to get the initial attention of a contact or a colleague is a critical skill for a High Trust Advisor and we can often do this by learning to forge our own unique message, what I call a PCR or PCE, a Point of Compelling Relevance or Engagement.

Gaining someone's trust means that we sometimes have to redefine our perceptions and our language when we work with others. More than ever, we have to start seeing what we offer from the other person's perspective and seek to understand the values that drive their decisions.

An example of this is our continuing dependence on old terminology when it comes to selling or persuading others for example, or when creating convincing proposals that we wish to pitch to a board or a team.

Most people are familiar with the term USPs', or *Unique Selling Points*. In fact, everybody in sales uses USP's. In fact, so many people use the same ones in similar industries and services that they are no longer *Unique* Selling Points rather they are *Generic* Selling Points!

For years we've talked about USPs or Unique Selling Points by which we could differentiate our offerings and make ourselves stand out to prospective contacts from the 'white noise' of competition. Regrettably the fact is that USPs *do not* make us stand out from the competition, they really only help to blend us in even further.

If we reflect on the USPs in any profession or industry can we honestly say that they are any different from what our competitors are also saying to the same prospects or what key decision makers have heard in previous proposals? Or do we sound exactly like our competitors or other colleagues pitching for budget or resources?

We provide 'solutions' or our 'experience' is second to none or we have 'one-stop-shops' or all the other *redundant terminology* that on any given day a person hears several times from different and equally uninteresting potential providers.

Yet USPs (Unique Selling Points) are still used by sales executives and professionals. However High Trust Advisors in sales positions use what I term 'Points of Compelling Relevance' (PCRs) and HTA in leadership now use PCE's (Points of Compelling Engagement) when pitching proposals.

A highly trusted advisor works on being memorable to the other person. They connect first with the other person's 'heart' and then to their 'head'. *By that I mean that they communicate emotionally first and then justify the emotional message with a logical reason afterwards.*

As I've said, they use what I term PCRs or *'Points of Compelling Relevance'.*

A PCR is a structured message that compels a person's attention because it is based on being emotionally compelling rather than simply appealing to a person's logic and thus sets our value proposition apart from everyone else.

Appealing to another person's emotion immediately captures their attention, makes us memorable to them and helps convince the client to spend their budgets with us or a key internal stakeholder to make decisions in favour of our proposals.

A *Point of Compelling Relevance* makes the listener want to act immediately on whatever it is that we are suggesting to them. It makes them want to sign up NOW or commit whatever they have for whatever it is that we are offering or proposing.

USPs (Unique Selling Points) on the other hand are based mainly on logic and so appeal primarily to the intellect or the reasoning ability of a person, it speaks to the surface of the proposal or the *logical* benefits available by considering the offering.

People then often *have to work out* or *think through* the value for themselves and as we live in a world of ever diminishing attention spans and work pressure, people just don't have the bandwidth or the interest to be bothered to do that and so, they don't. So much for our USP.

However, because a PCR/E speaks directly **to the emotions or the feelings of the decision-maker, where the benefit of the message is so relevant and so emotionally compelling,** they often decide immediately with their rationale being over-ridden by their immediate emotional response.

That emotion can be trust, power, control, money, time, profit, ambition, status, recognition but it is a *compelling* emotional trigger.

So now we can redefine 'selling' or 'leadership influence' as:

The ability to heighten the emotional state of a decision-maker so that we can influence their logical decisions for the transfer of goods, services, money, support or compliance for the mutual benefit of both parties.'

Of course, to create Points of Compelling Relevance/Engagement does require more thought and testing than simply using USPs. They also tend to be unique to a particular decision-maker or group of decision makers but the effect is immediate and unconditional. They buy or decide to act, now.

A case in point was my working with a bank's retail technology section who had been asked prior to the workshop to bring their USP's to the table. Their big USP was that "our credit card swiped twice as fast as any competitor".

Amazing. So, there was really only two questions I could ask about that. *"So what? What does that do for me?"* for which they had no answer.

However, by working it through (and identifying that their key accounts were major retailers) we identified that the PCR was that *'they could reduce queuing time for shop customers by 50%, improving the customer experience of the store and helping keep customers BECAUSE their credit card swipes twice as fast as any other'* (or they could also secure the transaction more quickly making it more secure).

Do you think that *resonated* with their up-market retail client? Improving the client experience, speeding up their transactions, enhancing security? *This* became the PCR that got them the access to and the attention of the client. Notice how the emotional value was placed first and *then* the logical justification for it.

Taking the time to work through the real value to the client or colleague that is buried deep within your industry or professional USPs allows us to uncover the language that most appeals to the emotional state of the decision-maker.

Once we discover the language that appeals to the person's 'heart' (in actuality their unconscious, which is the seat of their emotions), rather than their 'head' (or the conscious part of the brain, which is the seat of their logic and analysis) we then shape it into powerful suggestions that make us memorable in the heart and mind of the prospect.

We create our unique 'Points of Compelling' relevance or engagement.

For greatest effect the PCR/E language should be:

Concise. Kept short and to the point rather than a rambling statement.

Meaningful. Relate to the powerful and personal benefit or value that the decision-maker can gain from our offer.

Present Tense: The unconscious part of our brain responds best to instructions and suggestions made in the present-tense language rather than future tense such as 'you will' (This is often why many personal goals fail as people frame them using the words 'I will' instead of 'I am' or I want to').

Simple: The language is kept simple as the unconscious, and hence our emotional response, is faster to respond when we keep the language simple. (Imagine you are communicating with an 8-year-old).

The result of using a PCR/E is a much more engaged and attentive decision-maker, one who is both powerfully and emotionally influenced by our pitch or presentation right from the start.

PCR/E's help us to stand out from the other competitors chasing the market or seeking corporate influence and gets us access to and the attention of key decision-makers to unlock new revenue and opportunities.

Now that we have our 'PCRs' our next chapter deals with how we take them to our external and internal audiences.

17

4

The Secrets of Networking: How to Get Access to Decision-Makers

Being perceived as wanting to 'sell' or 'pitch' a product, a service, a project proposal (or even yourself) usually creates a 'perceived threat' in the mind of potential decision-makers and valuable contacts.

It is therefore important to create a favourable first impression and reduce the degree of resistance that we might otherwise be met with from internal decision-makers or business prospects.

We want to make sure that we create a safe and non-threatening impression of ourselves right from the very start of a relationship and start to build a compelling 'personal brand or executive presence' (what people say about us when we are no longer in the room).

This is important, as good business is built on permission and not on intrusion.

By far the most effective way, in my experience, of creating valuable and qualified business development and influential internal and external contacts, is personal contact networking.

Therefore for sales teams, professionals, executives and leaders who wish to be powerful and compelling influencers networking is not just an option, it is a professional requirement.

Why? Because in a world that is moving from old style 'command and control' and expertise-based models of leadership or business to a 'hybrid' model where *collaboration* is the key to success, then one's width and depth of contacts through your personal and professional network is a hugely valuable asset.

It is generally recognised that people who can create and leverage key relationships are the people who wield the power and influence in a new hybrid world where information and access to key people is critical.

Proactive networking can provide us with profile, position, presence, credibility, market knowledge and the many other benefits of being able to work comfortably and confidently within a room full of other professionals, key stakeholders, clients and decision-makers.

However having to 'work the room' (either in person or online) can also be an uncomfortable, fearful and even resentful feeling for many of us.

Like the negative stereotypical image of the 'sales person' we often associate 'good networkers' with brash, self-confident people, who can handle any rejection, muscle themselves in anywhere and take over a conversation to suit their own ends. Basically, people that are not nice to be around.

Most normal people would rather hug the wall, cradling our coffees until we have waited the allotted time and can mercifully escape from this room of people who all seem to know each other.

However professional networking is about strategy and fortunately, anyone can learn the strategy and the even better news for many people is that it's usually introverts (and not extroverts) that make the best networkers. Why? Because networking is all about the other person and not us. Extroverts tend to talk about themselves, introverts tend to want to listen to others.

Therefore the first thing about networking is to understand that networking is not about pitching our talents or our company's offerings (traditional 'selling') and the second thing is to understand that it's all about *asking permission.*

Remember *networking is not about us, it's always about the other person* and a good networker will spend time asking questions and actively listening to what the *other* person has to say.

Not only that but they will have reached this stage by having first gotten *the person's permission* to talk with them.

So what are the steps that get us speaking with not just anyone but the *right* person, the perfect decision-maker for our business or career influence needs?

1. Choose the Correct Event:

By this I mean select the event that is most appropriate to the profile of the decision-makers that we want to meet.

Where is the best place to meet your decision-makers? Obviously, at their own events. Just go to where they naturally gather to be together with each other. Seminars, conferences, lunches, dinners or internal company get togethers, town halls and BBQs. Attend webinars, online conferences where they specifically create networking rooms, even offer to present at webinars or better yet, organise your own and invite the people you really want to meet.

When we understand this simple rule (what we call 'the waterhole' or 'where do the animals come of their own accord' principle) then we can then start to choose the networking events we attend based on *profiling* or *niching* our decision-makers.

By profiling our existing contacts and dividing them into specific categories we can start to identify which contacts provide us with the most opportunities to give us the influence to get things done or buy our services or products.

We might niche people based on their industry or profession, their role, level of authority, professional or personal interests for example.

Once we understand this, it is now a simple matter of identifying their professional associations, their suppliers associations, technical conferences or indeed corporate events. In fact anywhere they are likely to gather for reasons other than being connected with us.

As an example, I once worked with a well-known international accounting firm and one partner, using this simple niching exercise discovered *26 additional places* where her ideal decision-maker profiles met. That's 26 new locations where she and her team could access their prospects and build new relationships.

However if we really want to excel at networking and establish as eclectic a network as possible my credo is simple *"wherever two or more are gathered together...there also shall I be"*.

Accept invitations to all events, plan them like a meeting and use them as tools to expand your network of contacts, decision-makers, referrers and influencers.

Think about invitations as 'door openers' where someone else has done all the work to get us in the room with our exact type of contact. An invitation to an event where everyone is a potential decision maker or referrer for us.

2. Target the People We Wish to See. Have an Objective:

The more specific we are about who we want to meet when networking the more successful we can be.

Plan out how many people we wish to meet (it's often best to go with a target of at least *three new contacts* per event). We can even plan to meet specific people who we know are at the event because of their value to us.

Ideally get the delegate list in advance from the event organiser (or get the attendee list when you get there as in Europe GDPR is making it more difficult to get a delegate list, however for your own company events that shouldn't be a problem.)

With the delegate list secured before we attend the event we can now target specific contacts and then perhaps research them first on their website, or set a Google Alert for information about their company or check LinkedIn which provides us with a photo and something about their background.

This can also help identify if we have any common connections or links who might provide us with an introduction.

...and it's not stalking ...its research!

Separately we might also categorise our potential contacts into decision-makers or as referrers (people who may not be able to make the decisions that can meet our needs but who can actively influence or connect you with the people who can).

3. Learn the Psychology of Groups

Conferences and seminars (online and offline) aren't just a big mass of people.

However next time we attend a live and in-person event we should take time to study the room before we launch ourselves into the fray.

Then we'll see that people in a 'live' environment arrange themselves in three distinct ways or what we call 'group dynamics'. They are:

A. *The Individual*

B. *The Open Group*

C. *The Closed Group.*

A. The Individual

They will be just like us, on the edge of the room looking for a way in.

They're wondering if they'll ever meet someone and how to go about it. They really want to connect with someone and if you make an effort to connect with them you will be welcomed with open arms. Remember why people come to networking events…to network!

To be accepted is the highest of human values. So if we offer a chance to connect to the Individual then in most cases he or she is highly likely to be delighted that we reached out to them.

B. The Open Group

This is a collection of individuals who are only just beginning to 'form and norm' as a group. They don't really know each other that well and so the group is arranged in a circle that has not yet closed so there is always a space for another person to join at any time. This is our space; all we have to know is the secret of the introduction.

The best kind of Open Group to join is a group made up of three people, especially if we can make up the gender numbers. This is an opportunity to get many different contacts at one go.

C. Lastly the Closed Group.

This group is best avoided because they know each other, they are in deep conversation, are already in rapport and are not 'open for business'. They don't want anybody else joining at this time.

Clever networkers know that by joining an Open Group they can close the group to others until such time as they have 'worked' the group and then they simply open the group again and disengage.

If the person you want to meet happens to be in a 'closed group' then don't despair, 'closed groups' will disperse eventually and that is now your opportunity to reach out and meet with your targeted contact.

Or indeed if you know someone well who is already inside the group approach them discretely and they will invite you to join the group, making a space for you to join them.

4. Making the Approach

So what is the magic formula that gets us 'invited in' to speak to all these people? It is simply courtesy and permission.

On making the approach to an Individual or an Open Group, we first make eye contact and smile!

When we smile we send a clear message to the other person's unconscious mind that we are harmless and therefore not a threat. (We humans cannot bite with our upper teeth alone i.e. therefore when the upper teeth are exposed we are communicating safety to the other person..)

Then we might ask ...*"Hi would you mind if I joined you?"* or *"May I join you?"*...then wait for the response (which will be positive) and then extend our hand to shake hands (another means by which humans install emotions and more emotionally effective than bumping elbows!) and join the person or group.

The key to engaging with anyone at an event is simply to request permission. Ask and you shall receive.

5. Ask Questions and Actively Listen

Many of us may have heard the phrase that in order to be interesting to people we must first be interested *in them*.

The very best way to keep people onside is to engage with neutral and open questions. These are questions that do not imply that a negative judgement will be made and are therefore seen as non-threatening.

A great way to start a conversation might be "What's your connection with the event?" or "What brings you here today?".

This neutral but universal question engages a person in a non-threatening way allowing us to quickly establish rapport by immediately giving control of the engagement to them and relaxing them into our company.

Key subjects to cover in a conversation might also would be have they travelled far, how did they get here, how are they finding the event and then once rapport is established, on to more professional matters.

Keep the conversation focused on them.

Techniques such as the structure that follows can help you learn to frame a conversation so that we are always on side with the person, yet at the same time gathering vital information for future contact.

This starts with:

1. What's your connection with the event?
2. Where have you come from? Have you travelled far?

3. Pastimes or interests ('so what do you do when you're not networking?' – usually ask about holidays, a neutral subject that can nevertheless be very engaging.)
4. Of course, we can also add Netflix or TV or movies to this list as well as a popular topic of neutral conversation and shared interest!

This kind of conversational structure ensures that:

1. We never run out of things to say and
2. The person we are speaking with feels both engaged and valued and that helps build rapport and trust.

When looking to spot business opportunities then also consider networking questions such as:

1. May I ask you who makes the decision regarding our service or product within the firm?
2. (If not the person you are speaking to) Are they also at the event?
3. Would you be happy to connect me with them?

These questions will evolve from when the other person quite naturally asks us 'what do *you* do?' However remember that the question in the mind of the other person when they ask you that is really **"what can you do for me?"**

So our answer must always have relevance and value.

By the way please don't take this as the chance to launch into your formal business presentation or sales pitch! This is the time for an 'elevator pitch' or a short intro to what we do and how it could help them, enough to catch their attention and interest.

All of this is leading up to the point where business cards can be exchanged and permission (that word again) sought to make a contact call and 'arrange a coffee' at a later date.

Alternatively, we can make excellent use of our cell or mobile phone to confirm meetings and connections as well, just ask them 'do you have your diary on your phone? Maybe we could set a time now if that's convenient?'

Such coffee meetings have the advantage of a 'warm contact' made at the event followed by permission to call and so normally meet with a greater chance of accomplishing your objective from the contact.

When they give us their business card and we have agreed a time to call, always note the time and date of the call on the card. This provides a 'visual anchor' for the person indicating that we intend to call at the agreed time.

This starts to create a 'double opt-in' with a contact. The first opt-in is where they have given you permission to call them to invite them to coffee.

The second 'opt-in' is where, making absolutely sure that we call them on the day and the time we promised, they agree to have coffee and set a date and time to meet either in person or online.

With the double 'opt-in' the other person is now perfectly aware that they are going to have a business conversation about their issues (or about our career or leadership proposal). They have invited us to engage, identify their critical challenges and then suggest a viable solution.

This is low-pressure, high-permission, networking.

There is also another simple but powerful strategy, that I call the **Advocate** strategy, for accessing more decision-makers using networking.

Many of us will have advocates or people who will happily speak on our behalf. People for whom our services or products or past efforts have provided significant value and for whom we have delivered on one of the four key Principles of Value that we influence people with:

1. We have saved them time.
2. We have saved them money
3. We have solved their problem
4. We have made them feel good

These advocates can serve as powerful sources of referrals for us provided we care for them.

Excellent advocates have two key features that define them: they have the POWER to help you and they have the DESIRE to help you.

I recommend that we list our advocates and create a strategy of advocate-care and contact: breakfast meetings, facilitating networking for them within the group, first access to reports, books based on their interests and so on.

Make sure that we also connect with them on a business social networking site. LinkedIn tends to be a network of choice when it comes to business social networks.

By using a social media site like LinkedIn we also get to see their second level of contacts, which are a rich source of potential referrals for us.

If you have used me and value what I deliver then you should be happy to refer me (as someone that you know can do the job) to your own personal contacts and friends for their benefit.

To help with that introduction, I would typically send a short email script that you could use and then you would email them (CC-ing me into the email) to put us in contact with each other.

I'm just looking for their permission to call them and get a meeting for coffee. Once I'm there it allows me to research their needs and look at areas that I can bring value to them.
If I can't, I move on and thank them for their time and of course, I've asked permission them to connect through LinkedIn if I haven't already.

If I'm referred to them via email from a trusted contact of theirs, this gives me a visibility and trust factor right from the word go leveraging an existing and trusted relationship.

Just like being introduced to someone at a 'live' networking event, I get their attention and a higher chance of getting to meet them.

But back to advocates. Invite them to coffee or lunch and while there ask them if they would be willing to introduce you to just three selected names that you have taken from their LinkedIn connections list.

The more advocates that we can create then the more personal referrals we get to have permission-based access to. Even 20 good advocates could mean over 60 new 'warm' referrals in any given year without ever having to make an unsolicited phone call or send an unsolicited email.

Obviously for a leader or executive who is not 'selling' but building a strong personal brand or executive presence within the business or industry the objective is different.

We would be looking for far less contacts so we want to use networking as a means of access to and attention of a smaller number of key stakeholders or advocates.

What becomes more important now for us is creating a regular 'contact strategy' with these contacts, remaining 'front of mind' with them by having coffees and lunches, or sending suitable reports or articles, perhaps books and continuing to network with them at corporate events and conferences or online.

5

Networking Hacks

In the previous chapter, we covered a practical understanding of networking and its value to a professional, executive or sales team in terms of creating the 'invitation to influence', positioning your brand within a wider company or building a list of new 'warm' prospects.

We looked at the psychology of groups, of individuals, the approach and the kind of questions that we might use to open a conversation.

Now I'd like to explore the rules of networking in a little more depth and explain how a simple conversation can be conducted to best effect and how to safely and ethically 'park' someone when you have accomplished your objective and want to move on from a conversation.

When entering a networking environment there are two things that one should keep in mind.

First, everyone you meet is connected by at least six degrees of connection.

That is, that theoretically someone knows someone, who knows someone, who will eventually lead you to the person that you want to meet anywhere on the planet. So we should value all connections.

Everybody in that room should matter to us. Why? Because if we have done our research correctly and have chosen the right room then everyone in that room is either a decision-maker or a potential referrer of business or a step on the path to getting in front of a desired contact.

In networking everybody matters and if we're in the right room, then the people you want to meet are no more than two degrees of separation from you so we should treat everyone with courtesy and respect. Remember your personal brand or presence can be defined as 'what people say about you when you are no longer in the room' and we want those comments to be consistently positive.

Secondly, every individual is there for the same reason as you, hoping to making connections that matter to them.

That means, that each person present is predisposed to meeting others and that each one of the people that we connect with are a link on a chain that can help us meet anyone else that we might wish to meet provided that we follow the chain.

Let's deal with the second point, first.

Every single person there has two things in common with us – 1. We both have some connection with the event and 2. We have both travelled from somewhere else to be there.

These are the two easiest things to talk about when we meet someone for the first time. When meeting someone and having made the approach and having once been accepted, we then have to ensure that we create rapport with that person.

Rapport is a sense of comfort and safety with others so our purpose therefore is to minimise any sense of threat that person may have about us, that may be heightened by any sense of difference between us and them. Therefore we always talk about neutral, open subjects and seldom if at all about business. Remember the ideal outcome from a networking event either live or online is to get a person to agree to a follow-up meeting or call.

By way of reminder from the last chapter, starting from the top, here are some sample questions to develop conversation with someone.

- What is their connection with the event?
- Have they travelled far to be here?
- What do they do when they are not working (hobbies and holidays) and finally
- Films or TV shows are usually a good topic to build rapport with too!

In between this of course, we need to qualify their value to us going forward.

We do this by using an 'elevator pitch' when they ask us what we do. Instead of instantly responding that we're 'an accountant' or 'an engineer' or ' a chief dishwashing technician' we ask a question that asks about their pain in business.

Of course we will have first researched the right question to ask by identifying the UPP (Universal Pain Point or the pain point most likely to be shared by most of the people in the room) for the people in that specific room.

This should be a part of our initial research attending any event and the reason why it is best to clearly profile (or niche) the room you want to be networking in.

Usually after they have answered the question 'what's your connection with the event ?', they then may ask us what do *we* do? That's when we have a chance to use my elevator pitch formula; *'Raise the Pain, then Position the Gain'.* Remember the underlying reason that they are asking 'what we do' is to really find out if we have any value for them and whether they should continue this conversation or not.

By way of example take an accountant at a small business conference. When asked what they do they might usually respond "I'm an accountant". To the small business owner their thinking is now "Well, I have one of those" meaning the accountant is not seen to be of any value and is now being dismissed for lack of value to the small business owner, who is now looking for a way out of the conversation.

An accountant who is trained to be a High Trust Advisor however would have said "Well, do you know the way that many small businesses struggle with access to credit to fund their businesses?" (most small business owners would tend to resonate with that challenge and nod in the affirmative).

By asking this question that is also positioning your understanding of their pain, you are identifying whether the listener responds positively or negatively to the problem being raised. If they do respond in the positive then they are a potential contact for us and we have a qualified a potential need.

If not, we might look to identify if they might be a referrer or if we want to keep our engagement short and move on to identify a more valuable contact.

However if the small business person does respond in the affirmative to this question, then the accountant might say "Well my business specialises in getting access to credit for small businesses".

Now the small business owner can definitely see a potential value in this new contact and this accountant then gets to hold their attention, their interest and possibly a business opportunity despite the fact that the business owner already has an accountant.

Note how much more effective it is to get people's attention when we demonstrate that we understand their pain and that we can offer a way to solve it. This is much more influential than simply saying what we do or who we work for.

Once we get a response which qualifies their interest (or lack of) we then store that information away and return to the conversation structure, sandwiching this qualifying or 'probing' process safely within what is otherwise a very neutral, non-pressurised, conversation. An affirmative response from the contact does not gives us permission to make a pitch. If anything it is even more important to focus on building the relationship now.

We continue to build the important foundations of having them get to know, like and trust us and only once that is done are we now ready to close the conversation and move on.

Now we might remind them of how we could help be of service or remove their pain from them and ask if they'd like to have a coffee sometime. We can ask them when would be best to call and then note these details on their card, plus where and when we met them.

An alternative close is to ask if they control their own diary i.e. do they set their own appointments? If so, ask them if they have their cell or mobile phone and just arrange a time for a coffee there and then with them, maybe also ask if you can send an invitation to connect on LinkedIn and then send an email afterwards to confirm.

We always ask for a coffee rather than a formal meeting because it is perceived as less threatening (I'm a great believer in 'hot coffees not cold calls'!) and less time consuming. It's only a coffee after all so there's little perceived threat on behalf of the other person.

Now we have permission for a meeting and a warm contact with whom we have made a positive impression on and who is happy to engage with us at a future time. This is the best kind of contact. Remember it is also *essential* to call exactly when you say you will. Your professional brand depends on it!

Once we have agreed a coffee meeting (or permission to call to arrange one) with this one contact we then need to move on (or as I call it 'Exiting Elegantly'!)

Our objective at a live networking event is to meet and get agreement from *at least* 1-3 people to have coffee with after the event is over. So we need to know how to move on from them to our next contact.

Moving on professionally requires attention too. It is essential that we treat everybody we meet with respect.

Because we are all connected, we do not know who the person we are speaking with is connected to. How we treat them may determine how we are treated in the future by a possible excellent business contact. So, we NEVER 'dump' people but we can 'park'.

In many cases when we have come to the end of a conversation at a live event people recognise that it has come to a natural end and are happy to part ways with us. However, sometimes a contact is determined to 'hang onto' us perhaps fearful that they will meet no-one else at the event if they let us go. Whatever the scenario we can easily and ethically disengage from such a persistent contact by giving them the option to leave us.

Try to never leave someone on their own when we move on, rather ensure that we have connected them with someone else. When someone feels that they have been abandoned by us they project that negative feeling onto us and are therefore not inclined to meet with us again.

First, just ask them *"I am going for a coffee...would you like to join me?"*

This might seem counter-productive but it is very important that we offer them an 'out' or an option to leave us to the other person. After all, they may also have been trying to get away from us and just didn't know how!

There will be one of two responses to our question:

1. They may say "No" as they themselves are happy to move on at that point to meet someone else.
2. They may say "Yes" in which case, we would then *both* move to get a coffee.

Along the way, we (as highly trusted advisors) quickly scan the room looking for an Open group ideally of three people. Once located, we steer toward the group; introducing both ourselves and our new friend to the group making the introductions where appropriate.

We have now introduced our original contact to new people, people they may never have met without our help. We have helped them further their connections within an event that, up to our helpful intervention, might have been a complete waste of time for them.

The Law of Reciprocity ensures that they may therefore work harder at a later date to help us (Law of Reciprocity: you do something for me and I feel obliged to return the favour only to a greater degree).

After we have identified and engaged our preferred contacts from this new group and once we have determined the most suitable time, we can then make our excuses and leave our original contact happily connecting with their new group of contacts.

It is simple, ethical and effective.

Networking is a requirement for all business professionals today. It is the means by which we build our networks of influence, our executive presence and valued brand both inside and outside of our organisations.

Anyone can learn the strategies to evolve into being a highly trusted and networked advisor. Remember, networking is a strategy not a hope.

6

How to Create Instant Trust and Rapport

Rapport is the key to successful relationships. Strong rapport means effective communication and creates the kind of high trust environment in which a person is open and willing to engage with us.

Exactly what rapport is has always been somewhat vague, many authors and trainers tend to gloss over it, somehow assuming that we should know instinctively how to create it.

That may seem to be a reasonable assumption. After all it *is* something we do quite naturally. But in assuming that we instinctively know *how* to create rapport, we miss an opportunity to understand *what* it is that creates an influential relationship.

The starting point in understanding rapport is to have a definition to work from. So, to help with this, I've outlined below a possible definition with which we can work:

Rapport is that *state* in human relations where there is an agreed, sometimes silent, *recognition and acceptance* of common issues.

One of the key words in that description is the word 'state' which can be defined as the *emotional* 'state' or 'feeling'. This positive 'state' or feeling *must* be present to have a highly trusted and influential relationship in the first place.

We cannot expect to create a compelling relationship in which we have a strong degree of positive influence unless we are first masters of building deep rapport with another person.

Imagine a situation where we meet someone for the first time. What is our initial emotional response? Are we immediately comfortable with them or are we little unsure at first, cautious or perhaps even a little suspicious?

It is perfectly natural for us to be a little uncertain of a person until such time as we have had a chance to assess them and their intentions. We have learned over millions of years to be cautious. Therefore, we seldom share our deepest secrets on first meeting someone. There is a process, mostly unconscious, which occurs within relationships as they develop.

However, it is also true that sometimes we instantly 'click' with some people, while with others we take and maintain an almost instant dislike to them. This is because at an unconscious level (and later at a conscious level) we have either positively or negatively been influenced by their appearance, their language, voice or behaviour and have sensed to a greater or lesser degree our shared or common issues.

In short, we have decided on the 'level of perceived threat' this person represents to us by virtue of how different or how similar they are to us. The greater the difference the more the level of perceived threat.

The greater the similarity the lower the level of perceived threat.

However, there are specific things that we can consciously choose to do to ensure that we create the strongest rapport possible with people and so establish high levels of trust, respect and influential communication with them. These I've captured in what I call the '7-Step Rapport Process'. By using the elements of this we can learn to quickly create deep rapport with other people.

Now, these are all things that we usually do unconsciously but by *consciously* understanding *what* we do and *when* to do them we can choose to use them in situations where we have to think about positively influencing a professional relationship right from the start.

It's also important to note that while this process is broken down into a series of steps, they all happen in the first few seconds or minutes of meeting someone for the first time.

Step 1: Discounting

Within seconds of meeting another person everybody begins the unconscious process known as 'Discounting'.

This is where we start to 'mark down' people depending on their appearance, voice, body language etc. For each of us, **we** are the most 'perfect' person in our world and as a result we tend to compare everyone else *using ourselves* as the benchmark.

This process comes from our need to find out whether this person is a threat to us or safe to be with and this need for assessment is 'hard-wired' into our brains from early in the development of mankind and is totally unconscious. It is only afterwards that we rationalise consciously the decisions that we make.

This threat-level assessment process has a direct effect on the level of rapport that we establish with another person and ultimately on the level of influence that we can exert on them and them on us.

This is why things like dress, appearance, accent and body language have an important place in building rapport as they are the initial points of reference that people use to determine their response to us.

The 'secret' of rapport and trust is truly simple: *'People Like People Who Are Like Them.'*

As a result, the more like the other person I can *appear* to be, the more likely they are to like me and feel safe and comfortable in my presence. To be a successful and highly trusted advisor in any circumstance, we need be able to adapt successfully to many different personality styles and how we this we'll explore in detail in a later chapter.

By the time 'Discounting' has been completed and the next stage begins we have unconsciously critiqued the person we have just met and moved to Step 2.

Step 2: *Judgement*

At this point we chose which 'box' they go into. Humans need stereotypes to help them process the vast amount of information we receive whenever we meet someone for the first time.

We have 'psychological templates' based on our past conditioning that other people are either good or bad, attractive or not etc. and a great many of our relationships are based on this stereotyping or generalisation. It's one of the ways in which we process the vast amounts of information we receive every day and learn.

It's used extensively in film and TV as a means of being able to tell the story in a short time period. Can't we always tell the good guys from the bad guys in movies and soap operas sometimes just by their dress or body language? This allows our brain to 'fill in' the information about a character without the need for a detailed 'back story' every time. Unfortunately, it is also used by darker elements in society to foster division by an 'us and them' mentality and to create fear.

Of course, the importance of understanding the power of rapport is being aware that while we are doing this to others, they are also doing it to us. It's useful to remember that judgement is a two-way process!

Therefore, it is essential that our rapport-building skills are such that we are always assured of being marked in the upper percentile in other people's judgements. A low judgement in another person's eyes can limit our ability to influence them.

Within a few minutes (and sometimes just seconds) of 'first contact' other people have decided whether or not we are a credible person or professional and so this is where we sow the seeds for a successful business relationship or not.

Step 3: Eye Contact

One of the first things that we notice when meeting someone is their visual appearance and a good visual appearance can often score major bonus points while communicating.

First, appearance is important. Suitable dress (appropriate to the circumstance), general hygiene, style of hair etc. all help with the initial impact we make.

While we cannot always expect to be perfectly turned out on all occasions, remember that our clothes and general appearance reflects our professional or even social status and credibility.

More subtly (but importantly) eye contact (or the lack of it) is also considered during the discounting process. Poor eye contact turns people off. It communicates poor (or lack of) interest in the other person. No one likes to be 'overlooked' so they in turn reflect that back to us and exhibit a low level of interest in us, hardly the best way to start an influential relationship.

In general, we should always maintain good eye contact when we meet someone new. There is much to be said for having a good, open and honest gaze. The eyes are the windows of the soul and we can communicate very powerfully with just our eyes when we flirt with someone for example or look skywards to portray exasperation.

That said, for some of us it can be difficult to maintain eye contact without staring. This can be awkward as staring at people directly can often portray aggression or potential confrontation and that most definitely will not assist us with developing good rapport.

In general, we create safe, neutral and yet effective eye contact when we keep our gaze anywhere within an inverted triangle, with the apex ending at the point of the chin and the base of the triangle between the person's eyes.

Keeping our gaze anywhere within this imaginary triangle will help us maintain good, neutral and engaged eye-contact of a non-confrontational nature, that then helps keep the other person's interest and attention on us.

Step 4: The Handshake

We often assume a lot about a person from their handshake and that often determines our level of rapport.

A handshake can install positive or negative emotions in someone about us as soon as 'first contact' is made. As most of our decisions are emotionally based, we need to ensure that the 'first' feelings people experience about us are as positive as possible.

For example, how do we feel when we get that loose, limp, 'wet fish' disinterested handshake that hardly passes as a handshake at all? Or what about the 'earthquake' where the hand is seized and squeezed in a vice-like grip?

Sometimes the other person may attempt to dominate the handshake (and hence the relationship) and their hand will be very prominently placed, palm downwards, on top of ours, deliberately (although probably unconsciously) placing us in a submissive position. They may even extend their hand with theirs pointing downwards, forcing us to place our hand underneath theirs.

To counteract this, all we have to do is cover the top of their hand by grasping it briefly with our other hand, so that we end up enclosing their original handshake in our two hands! Now who's in charge and we have given a clear sign that we intend to conduct our business and relationship as equals.

However, we can also use this in our favour.

By being the first to engage someone by extending *our* hand *palm upwards* in the 'submissive' position we immediately place the other person in a 'dominant" (and therefore more secure and 'in control') position.

Their immediate feelings are therefore of being in control, safe and as a result their initial anxiety or initial sense of threat is lessened as is their potential resistance to us.

Step 5: The Power of Your Smile

Smiling is critical when meeting someone for the first time. It conveys an attitude of openness and acceptance to the person, helping them to relax and to be open to us in turn. Think of the last time you met someone, were they smiling or not?

How did it make you feel the last time you met someone who smiled as if delighted to meet you? Now think of how that makes others feel when *you* smile when you meet them.

For ourselves, it helps us to relax and places us in a positive state which makes it easier for us to manage the communication. The better and more relaxed we feel the easier the conversation will be. In addition, our expectations of the success of the conversation will be high. Such expectations cause a reciprocal effect from the other person and hence the process tends to be successful.

The single greatest human need is that of being *accepted* and it is conveyed easily and effortlessly with the power of our smile. Smiles are infectious too they just seem to spread good cheer and warmth into a relationship.

Smiling comes from the fact that by exposing our upper teeth we are indicating that we cannot attack, primarily because (as humans) we cannot grasp with our upper teeth alone.

However, if we stick out our chin and expose our lower teeth, we are indicating hostile intention. Ever notice someone getting aggressively hostile? They immediately stick out their chin, don't they? They unconsciously intend to 'take a bite' out of us. So, smile!

It's gives us the advantage when communicating with others and smile also with your whole face, not just your teeth. There's nothing worse than an insincere smile. It's an effort to create and does not help the relationship in any way. People know whether we are being sincere or not.

From a more technical point of view a genuine smile can be distinguished from a forced one because the muscles that move the face to smile and cause those 'crow's feet' or 'smiling eyes' only contract when people are expressing the true emotion of happiness.

Smiling can save us great points on the discounting scale and it's fun to do.

Step 6: Influential Questions

As a business professional who is becoming a highly trusted advisor, it's important to remember that *the person who controls the questions is the person who controls the conversation.*

It's also important to remember that, in general, people love to talk about themselves. *They* are *their* favourite subject so *let* them be. It's not often that we get an attentive audience and people tend to like the opportunity to talk about ourselves. We also tend to think very favourably about the people who listen actively to *our* stories.

So, ask them questions. It's a powerful rapport-building tool. It enhances the other person's feeling of safety with you as the person they are hearing doing most of the talking is themselves and who do people feel the safest and most comfortable with - themselves!

Questions maintain attention, allowing us to identify the triggers by which people make their decisions, the values that they consider important; they allow us to install ideas, explore, change a person's perception. They are the ultimate influencing tools.

We'll cover the area of questions in far greater detail a little in the chapter on advanced questioning skills.

Step 7: Body Language

Body language lends a great deal to the *congruence* (when what we are feeling is what is being expressed in our voice and body language) and the perceived sincerity of our message. People will always look at our body language before they listen to our spoken words and will act on this first when it comes to making decisions about the truth of your message.

If, for example, we are stretching and yawning while at the same time telling people how wonderful it is to be here with them and how exciting we find their company they're not likely to be convinced of the sincerity of our message are they?

Therefore, a great deal of the sincerity of the message will be tied up in how our body is reacting (or not) to the people with whom we are communicating. Body language is too great a subject to explore here but here are some simple tips:

Tip 1: Be aware of your distance from the other person, breaching a person's privacy barrier will cost you points on the rapport scale. Too close and they may feel intimidated (of course after Covid19 I think we can get a little closer than 2 metres!)
However, some people have a need for a great deal of space between themselves and others in order to feel comfortable, so noting how far or how close they come when shaking hands with you can give an indication of what's a comfortable distance for them and what's not

Tip 2: Touching another person can sometimes help to anchor encouragement or praise.

However the body has 'neutral' and 'intimate' areas that we must be aware of. For example, the arm from elbow to shoulder is often considered 'neutral' or acceptable area of touch for some people but the arm from elbow to hand is not and touching it may be considered intimate and inappropriate.

Tip 3: Mannerisms: Mannerisms are those unconscious habits which we all have to some extent.

They are not just physical but can also be verbal. For example the person who continually ends each sentence with the words "eh?" or "you understand" or "actually" or "you know" or some form of words of which they are totally unaware but which the listener is getting increasingly tired of hearing.

Tip 4: Mannerisms can also be physical, the constant tapping of a foot or finger for example. In each case they should be identified and removed from our physical behaviour.

But how do we remove something that is unconscious?

Pluck up the courage to ask our partner or spouse the things they notice about us. I could guarantee that the things they notice and are willing to comment on are the same things strangers and work colleagues notice and say nothing about but file away when it comes to their opinion about you.

Tip 5: Posture: Posture, or the way our bodies stand or sit or lie, often reflects our inner state or how we are feeling at any time.

For example, travelling to work on a Monday morning, do we notice the posture of most people passing us by or sitting on Zoom calls? Usually unhappy about returning to a job they no longer enjoy or find interest in, they tend to have a 'hang-dog' look about them. Their heads are down, their bodies slumped.

But notice these same people on a Friday afternoon. Work is over for the week. They're laughing, heads high and looking forward to time for themselves. Their bodies are reflecting the up-beat mood that they are experiencing internally. Sports people often use 'physical determination techniques' going through a series of exercises prior to a game to get both their minds and bodies ready for the athletic challenge ahead.

So, in the process of communication with other people, what state should we ideally be in - upbeat or depressed? Can't we often tell how someone feels just by the way they appear?

We need to become more aware of our own body language and the message that it's communicating to the people with whom we wish to communicate successfully. People want to engage with people who generate a sense of confidence in and comfort with themselves. So, by being more aware of our body language and how we can use it can help us send a powerful and unconscious message to those around us.

Body language too plays a part in the processes of matching and mirroring.

Matching and mirroring are the means by which we reflect back to people their own postures and actions. The purpose behind this is to indicate that we are like them and so we are 'safe'.

Remember the 'secret' of rapport, that people like people who are like them? Therefore, the more we can consciously match the physical behaviour of others that we want to influence (the more like them we appear to be) the more 'likeable' we can appear to them. *Matching* is the process by which we exactly copy the actions of the people with whom we are communicating.

As a very simple example, if we are facing someone and they raise their left hand, then we raise our left hand. If they cross their legs, then we cross our legs. It's very similar to the game children play that drives adults crazy when they do it to us.

Mirroring is similar to matching in that we wish to convey like behaviour, but the difference is that instead of moving exactly like the other person we now move in the reverse.

If they move their left hand, then we move our right, if they move their right leg, we move our left.

The purpose behind this is that we now appear to the other person as if we were appearing as their reflection in a mirror to them and therefore appear to be doing exactly what they do.

This can create very deep rapport indeed even to the extent that the person may believe that the words that we use are their own thoughts!

But a word of caution: the secret behind matching and mirroring is that they must be done out of the level of the other person's conscious awareness and *out of synch* with their movements and never at the same time as the other person.

Ever notice kids doing it to us and it drives us crazy? So how would adults feel if they notice us doing it to them? This is called 'mimicking', not an appropriate use of body language!

There is sufficient knowledge in the public arena available to people to know why we might want to Match and Mirror them and no one likes to feel they are being manipulated. So, if it's obvious that we are doing it, what are the likely consequences?

Timing and subtlety are therefore crucial in applying Matching and Mirroring techniques.

So here are some useful guidelines for Matching and Mirroring:

1. Match and Mirror the Parts of the Body that You and the Other Person See.

There's no benefit in Matching or Mirroring if the other person cannot see the actions as if it does not register, it's wasted.

2. Actions Should Be Offset by Timing

If people are using their hands when speaking to us, stay still. When they stop speaking and when we start to speak, then we can Match that action. Likewise, if they lean forward, take your time, then say something and lean forward to match the posture of the other person.

Using your voice as a distraction can often help mask the fact that you are shifting your body language.

They are both focused on and distracted by what we are saying and generally will not consciously notice that we are using (or 'feeding back') their gestures to them.

3. Pace, Pace, Lead, Lead

This is how we can identify if we are generating rapport with someone.

Pacing is when we are *following* the actions of the other person. We would continue to do this until such time as we get a sense or a feeling that we are in rapport.

To test this, we would then change the pattern of pacing by moving or making a gesture of our own or using words that are unique to us. If the other person then follows us, we are in rapport and we can then *lead* that person through our own gestures and movements or language.

As long as the other person then continues to follow our lead, they will be open to the suggestions or ideas that we wish to present to them

4 . Rapport with Two or More People

When generating rapport with more than one person, it is sometimes necessary to focus on one while Matching or Mirroring the other(s). The person that you want to Match or Mirror should be the most dominant one within the group.

You can Match or Mirror the dominant person's actions, voice or words while paying specific attention to the other people in the group. By doing this we are generating rapport in two ways.

First, we are creating 'first level' rapport with the dominant member of the group through posture. This should bring them unconsciously into rapport with us and thus into agreement with what we are suggesting.

This person is unaware of our actions because we are not directly facing them or perhaps only occasionally addressing them, while we appear to concentrate our attention on the other people in the group.

By doing so we are then taking on some of their authority within the group by appearing to the group members to be like the dominant person.

This then can lend authority to our communication with the other members of the group because we are now communicating with the 'traits' of the dominant group member or through 'second level' rapport.

5 . Positioning

Another important aspect is the way we position ourselves when we seek to Match or Mirror people. Where possible, we should try to avoid sitting directly opposite someone. Instead, we should move our chair so that it is at a near 45-degree angle to the person with whom we are seeking to create rapport.

This has two effects. One, it appears less confrontational than when facing someone directly and two, it limits their perception of the fact that we may be Matching or Mirroring their movements and actions.

Remember, we only get one chance to make a first impression. Therefore, professional communicators and advisors use all the tools at our disposal to ensure that our first impression is the very best possible. Good 'First Contact' with another person can make all the difference in creating a long-term, influential and mutually profitable business relationship.

Once we have made 'first contact' the next stage is now how to consciously deepen the level of rapport.

The next step is learning how to work with the unique personality types that we meet every day and by learning to be able to 'flex' our communication style or 'preference' to appear more like the other person, we can learn to deepen trust and maximise influence.

It's time for 'Connecting in Colour'.

7

Connecting in Colour

Imagine a situation where, within a few minutes of meeting a person, you could recognise their preferred way of communicating, be able predict the way they were likely to respond to us and then adapt our own responses to match theirs and thus create powerful and deep rapport and trust?

Think of the benefits.

One could *choose* exactly how to respond to them, *match* their exact preferred communication style, know *how* to feed them information in the *specific way* in which they process information, know *exactly* how quickly they were likely to make decisions and what makes them *comfortable* when communicating.

As a Highly Trusted Advisor, we go beyond just communicating a message. We have the ability to *connect* with, to *influence* and to *engage* others at a deeper level as this is what can determine the level of our influence with any given prospect, client, colleague, team member or key stakeholder.

Understanding the psychology behind connecting with others gives us a powerful means of creating rapid rapport and deepening trust. This chapter introduces a highly effective (and fun) model for communications excellence based on the many 4-Quadrant behavioural systems that are available in the market as psychometric and training tools today.

For centuries, philosophers have identified four broad types of personality. Over 2,500 years ago the Greek philosopher and medical pioneer Hippocrates was the first to be credited with 'typing' human behaviour and providing the first colour system which we still draw from today.

The eminent psychotherapist Carl Jung further developed this idea in the 20th century and added his own concepts on how we focus our energy, make decisions and whether we are 'big picture' (global) thinkers or specific (detailed) thinkers.

Jung suggested that we have the capacity for all kinds of personality traits or energies within us but that we have a *'preference'* for exhibiting certain traits above others.

It is this balance of energies or personal traits (or 'functions' as he called them) that makes each of us unique and while we may share some (or even many) traits with others, we are all unique creatures, with unique preferences.

The full range of psychological types can be depicted (as per Hippocrates) as a circle with four key colour quadrants - Red, Yellow, Green and Blue. All of us have one of these as a 'dominant colour preference' that gives us a preferred style of thinking, working and interacting with others.

Each colour preference or personality type has its own unique strengths and weaknesses, depending on the situation and the perspective of others.

There is also sometimes a slightly less dominant (but still strong) colour preference, or a secondary colour, which can also impact significantly on our behavioural style.

To make matters even more interesting, when mapped using a psychometric profile we can see that most of us can have *two* distinct styles of personality.

We have an *'unconscious'* style or preference that is our natural self or *'who we are when we are not thinking about who we are'*, our 'unmasked selves' or what I sometimes call our 'default' self. This is often what family and close friends see (or indeed what we revert to when we are stressed or under pressure).

Then we have our *'conscious'* self that is the 'mask' or the communication preference style that *we choose to project to others when we go to work*.

These personality preferences come down to how the colours interact with each other, some being closely aligned and others being polar opposites.

The real secret is in recognising that the traits are not opposite but actually **complement** each other and a successful leader or sales professional can recognise this and use it to their advantage and that of the person they wish to influence by creating a close, compelling and open relationship.

Now let's look at the four key prominent colours or personality types and the traits that we can associate with them:

WARRIOR REDS tend to be direct and up-front, quick to make decisions and very focused.

They come across as the most seemingly confident of the colours having a high degree of 'inner certainty' that means that once they are happy with an idea, they seldom look to others for affirmation that it's the right thing to do. They just do it.

They are very determined and love to face a challenge. Being action-oriented they tend to *'reflex rather than reflect'*, which works for them but can be quite a challenge for other colours.

They can be very articulate and tend to be 'big picture' thinkers, not great on the detail but very good at creating the vision or the mission.

To their opposite colour however (Healer *Green*) they can often appear as aggressive or arrogant, not waiting for feedback and guilty of pushing others too hard.

Warrior Reds would be considered negatively by Healer Greens as a poor listener, confrontational and not waiting for feedback or valuing the contribution that others make.

Some Healer Greens might even consider a Warrior Red to be a 'bully'. What lies behind this perception however has to do not just with the preferred values of the Red but also their *style of communication*.

With Warrior Reds being 'Visual' communicators, they 'see' things and as a picture paints a thousand words, they feel that they have to describe everything they see when communicating with others the detail of what they are seeing.

As they 'see' a new mental image every nanosecond this is a lot of information that has to be transmitted quickly, (usually through speech) meaning that they can often *overwhelm* people who do not process in pictures but in some other form of modality (such as Healer Greens who process information by *feeling or touch*).

Warrior Reds often benefit from slowing their pace of speech and learning *to ask more question* and *make more suggestions* and allowing others to have the chance to engage with them.

Equally, when we are communicating with a Warrior Red, we need to speed up our own pace of speech. Only then can the Warrior Red receive the information at a speed that they can create the mental images necessary to make sense of what we are saying to them.

In fact, it is by learning to be able to *flex* our *preferred communication style* that we connect most successfully with the other colours.

This may seem uncomfortable and requires some effort on our behalf, especially when dealing with an opposite colour but it does help significantly to make the other colour more comfortable with us, bringing down barriers, lessening threat, increasing their capacity to engage and making them ours to influence.

The values, or decision-making motivators, of a Warrior Red tend to be power, status, ambition and control.

For Warriors 'control' is an important value and they often need to see that we are 'in control' of things when we work with them as advisors or team members.

If we fail to keep them 'in the communications loop' on things, if we fail to let them 'see' us regularly (even just popping in and updating them on things) they quickly move to micro-managing us fearful that we (and so they) are not 'in control'.

Some people fear challenging the opinions of Warrior Reds, believing this will lead to confrontation or aggression. In fact, most Reds positively welcome 'push back' especially if it adds to the information that allows them to get the task or the mission done.

Therefore, when confronted by a Red stand your ground and be firm on the facts. However, to avoid confrontation try not to challenge them for their sense of position or power.

Warrior Reds can make very good clients if you're a sales advisor. Usually they have the authority (as their ambition moves them up the ladder) and they make decisions quickly. Once the decision is made, they tend to stick with it.

We just need to keep our presentation and meetings short, positive and focused on the subject. The most effective strategy for influencing them is simply to let them think it's their idea!

Tips for recognising a Warrior Red are:

1. Extroverted and tend to speak at a fast pace.
2. Task (not People) Focused, interested in logic, data, and accom-

plishing the mission.
3. Global or 'Big Picture' thinkers.

INFLUENCER YELLOWS are highly sociable and love the concept of fun, recognition and variety.

Fun and interacting with others are key parts of their personality and they tend to be happy to spend lots of time with visitors. They can be demonstrative, enthusiastic and very expressive, often finding their way into creative and media industries, sales or marketing and event management roles.

Like Warrior Reds, they are extroverted and articulate but less well organised or focused.

In fact, meetings with Influencer Yellows will tend to last longer than any of the other colours as they love to chat about everything and anything and often need to be (gently) brought back time and again to the point of the conversation!

Influencer Yellows process information through *sound* and as a result are not great readers. They prefer to communicate *through conversation rather than writing*.

They are quick to build relationships and can often be seen as 'sociable' and 'the life and soul of the party'. To the extent that if they walk into a room and there is no-one else there to talk to then they are likely to end up talking to the wall as they just can't help expressing themselves!

Rather than giving them long written proposals or reports, Influencer

Yellows would prefer to be *talked through* the proposal or report, their primary processing modality being auditory or sound.

They are highly adaptable and people-focused but tend not to be good at organisation, planning or detail, so not great at following instructions or rules. Similar to the Warrior Reds they are Global thinkers great with the origination of an idea, often highly creative but they tend not be very good completer/finishers of projects.

As a result, they may travel down many pathways with us but getting them to make a final decision to buy or commit to a project can be a challenge. Without arranging to walk (and talk) them through a proposal, this same proposal may sit in the 'in' tray and never be looked at again!

They also tend to make decisions quickly and then either forget they made the decision or fail to follow-up.

Their buying or decision-making values tend to focus on fun, recognition and variety.

For them their greatest challenge is in communicating with the highly reflective, detail-focused Scholarly Blues.

Scholarly Blues tend to see Influencer Yellows as excitable, frantic and even indiscreet (!) and can be challenged when dealing with their upbeat and outgoing natures. A Yellow might find a Blue cold and reserved, unwilling to engage and become part of the group, preferring their own company.

Personal recognition and affirmation can be a great motivator for the

Influencer Yellow and they can be most open to corporate entertainment as they like 'to see and be seen'.

Tips for recognising an Influencer Yellow are:

1. Extroverted, as they display strong extroverted behaviour and speak in a medium to fast pace.
2. People Focused (unlike the Reds who are Task focused), interested in how people feel and figure in the scheme of things.
3. Global or 'Big Picture' thinkers.

Next, our **HEALER GREENS** are tremendous listeners and highly supportive of others.

Being of service to other people is important to them and they can be patient, polite and pleasant to all that they meet. They are caring and encouraging of others, somewhat reserved, patient and relaxed and are often great team members.

They process information through how they *'feel'* about things, and such a modality means that they can often *take longer to make decisions* as they need the time to reflect on their physical feelings about an idea or a proposal.

Healer Greens can be slower to respond to a question or a suggestion as they process the information *kinaesthetically* (through feeling), wanting to be *comfortable* with any response before they give it.

This can often frustrate a Red, or even a Yellow, who are used to making quick decisions and want things to move along quickly to suit *their* preferred communication style.

A Healer Green may find the Warrior Red arrogant and aggressive as the Red's sense of inner certainty, confidence and task focus are at odds with the Green's more collaborative and team-based style.

The way a Healer Green *feels* about things is very important. The worst thing that one could do is to force a Green into making a decision without allowing them the time to 'get a feel for it'. Doing so can result in the Healer Green preference person being so uncomfortable that they could cancel an order or contract or even end a business relationship.

I recommend that before a meeting with a Healer Green where a decision might be required, that all relevant and written documentation be sent to them *ahead of any meeting* to allow them to review, get a feel for it and comfortable with it and prepare for the face-to-face meeting.

For Greens their key values, around which they would base their decisions, would be loyalty, trust, transparency, stability, security and comfort.

As we can see from these values, they are not people who are quick to change providers, jobs or teams and would only do so if they feel very 'uncomfortable' or 'uncared for' with and by the existing provider or team leader.

For Healer Green's the quality of the relationship is critical. They are highly people-focused and want to be valued and listened to.

Tips for recognising a Healer Green are:

1. Introverted, as they display relatively introverted behaviours. They tend to speak at a slower and reflective pace, seeming a little reserved towards others in early interactions.
2. People Focused, (unlike the Reds who are Task focused), interested in how people feel and figure in the scheme of things.
3. Specific thinkers, (focused on the small details and the specifics).

Lastly, **SCHOLARLY BLUES** are highly analytical, reflective, thoughtful people who like to make decisions based on a deep understanding of the situation or third-party data.

They are the kind of person who prefers to reflect and seek to understand even the smallest of details before committing to any decision. This can mean that not only are they slow to confirm or make a decision, but they can be seen as strong procrastinators often waiting too long to make decisions.

Once they make a decision then they are absolutely committed to it and are very unlikely to change it, so they often make excellent long-term clients and excellent administrators and planners.

They tend to process information through what we call an 'Auditory Digital' process. In its simplest form this means that they like to have a conversation in their own head about things before they talk to the person actually in the conversation with them!

This is why the Scholarly Blues are sometimes called 'low reactors' in relationships, remaining silent and reflective and allowing the other person to do the talking. In fact, they *are* having a conversation but with *themselves*.

They love getting their information in writing preferring to analyse information and one cannot provide them with enough data.

Their values are competence, credibility, organisation, stability, systems and planning and they are very comfortable with numbers, often making excellent administrators, accountants, engineers, technical people, actuaries and so forth.

They will ask (a lot of) questions and as *credibility* is a key value for them it is important that *we* are well versed in our subject matter or bring someone with us to the meeting who is, as they will ask very technical and detailed questions. No point asking them to read the manual by the way, they probably wrote it.

There is no way that we can expect to muddle our way through a meeting with them. If we don't have the information or can't answer the questions they will quickly switch off and will see you as wasting their time.

Like the Healer Greens, but even more so, it is a useful strategy to send a lot of written information in advance of any meeting and then email them to request a list of questions they would like us to address during the meeting itself.

This kind of pre-meeting preparation will ensure a much more favourable response from the Scholarly Blue and ensure that we get to a positive decision sooner.

Tips for recognising a Scholarly Blue are:

1. Introverted as they display relatively introverted behaviours. They

tend to speak at a slower and reflective pace, seeming quite reserved towards others in early interactions even more so than a Green.

2. Task Focused (unlike the Yellows who are People-focused), interested in logic, data, rationale and the task or measurable objective.
3. Specific thinkers (very focused on the small details and the specifics).

When we understand the principles of this colour model we can move to a world of 'glowing rainbows of colour' thus quickly becoming able to recognise, adapt and build high levels of trust and influence with our clients or key stakeholders.

Success in today's world is about a different set of values from than those that mattered in the past.

Now the values of business are collaboration, co-creation, connection and community and all of this begins with our ability to act with greater awareness or consciousness when we meet others. This is the mark of a highly trusted advisor, communicator and influencer.

8

Advanced Questioning and Influencing Skills

As children nothing came more naturally to us than the powerful "WHY?" question.

"Why is the sky blue Daddy?". "Because the angels painted it that way love". "Why is the grass green Daddy?". "Because the angels painted it that way munchkin." "Why did the angels paint it that way?". "I don't know sweetheart - go ask your mother..."

Questions are powerful tools for influential communication. They can install ideas in people's minds, change their perception of problems and help us to gain compliance or agreement to our suggestions.

To be a highly trusted advisor it's important for us to remember that *the person who controls the questions is the person who controls the conversation.* It's also important to remember that, in general, people love to talk about themselves. *They* are their favourite topic. So, let them.

Ask questions because questions are a powerful rapport and trust-building tool.

Get other people actively involved in the conversation and more importantly, get them involved in conversations where they are *co-designing* or *co-creating* their own solutions.

The more the other person is involved in solving their own problems (with our help) then the more ownership they take of the solution, the easier they are to influence and the less likely they are to walk away from a proposal or a plan that we build together.

Another key reason for using questions is that when a person is looking to answer our question, it is at that moment, more than any other moment in the conversation, that they are focusing their full attention, involvement and engagement on us, on our project proposal or on our sales offering.

They are just not thinking about *anything* else at that time and they can't resist the images that we are planting in their mind.

Now let me share 5 primary types of influential questions that we can use to manage and guide any and all meetings.

The most common types of questions used within the influencing and engaging process are the:

1. Open and Closed Questions

The Open question is one that encourages a person to talk. It is designed to gather information, opinions, thoughts and ideas.

The English writer Rudyard Kipling had a little verse that summed up the key forms of Open questions: *"I had six honest serving men and they served me true. Their names were How, What, Why, Where, When and Who".*

By using these six 'open' question types we can gather enormous amounts of information from people during the course of a single conversation whether of a business or personal nature.

Open questions however can often be answered by unqualified or unspecified answers. For example, "how many people are coming to the meeting?" might be answered by "a few" or "about ten".

However, by using the word **'specifically'** in any 'open' question this ambiguity can be removed every time. "How many people, ***specifically***, are coming to the meeting?" might be answered by "the CEO, CTO and CFO" or "exactly 5 people".

This is an important point because wherever ambiguity or lack of clarity exists in a conversation it leaves us at a disadvantage. Lack of clarity in a business conversation may allow the client, prospect or contact to come back at us at a later time and maybe cancel the business or agreement and a lack of clarity in a leadership or management conversation can impact on the performance of the individual as they leave the conversation confused and uncertain.

Closed questions on the other hand are designed to elicit either a 'Yes' or 'No' answer. They are not designed to encourage conversations. They are designed to get confirmation or denial of information.

These questions are typically *Did, Is or Are?*

Having now looked at the most basic open and closed questions here are some examples of more sophisticated types of questions.

2. Tag Questions

Tag questions are questions that can be added to the end of a sentence, buried in the middle of a sentence or hidden at the start of a sentence, and they are used to elicit a positive response, or "yes" answers, from people.

I mean, if you were to ask a person for a positive answer you could, couldn't you? Wouldn't you?

If you wanted to don't you think you could just get a positive answer by asking a simple question? Of course, you could, couldn't you?

Words like 'wouldn't, can't, don't, shouldn't, doesn't' and so on are ideal tag questions and such questions are usually used *after a suggestion to take an action has been made using an Open question*, aren't they?

First the suggestion...followed by a tag question...that receives the affirmative (yes) response and confirms the suggestion as agreeable to them.

"Perhaps we could just *get the paperwork out of the way*? That would be worth considering *wouldn't it?*"

3. Preferential or 'Double-Bind' Questions

Preferential or 'double-bind' questions pre-suppose that the listener once presented with the question, accepts the offer or the outcome inherent in (or built into) the question. It's just a question of *which* option they are choosing to get to that outcome.

For example, "would you like to go now or in 30 minutes?" pre-supposes that the individual *is* going, even though they may not have considered it *before* the question was asked. They have a choice over *when* but not *if* (hence the 'double-bind' – "now" or in "30 minutes").

"Would you like me to call tomorrow or the next day – which would you prefer?" is a useful and common preferential question for setting up appointments.

Such questions involve an outcome that works in our favour, regardless of which option the listener chooses to meet the outcome. We control the outcome, but they have a choice over which option to take. Regardless of which option they chose however it always leads to the same outcome.

This is important as offering too many options or choices to another person can be confusing and lead to delay. Offer them two but not more than three options at the most at any time. Usually, people will choose the middle of three options and anything over three options they tend to defer the decision on as they reach overwhelm.

3. Exploratory Questions

Exploratory questions are a development of the Open question type.

They are very useful when we are seeking clarification on (or further information about) the subject raised by another person, or in answer to a question from another person by which we have been momentarily confused or caught off guard.

The question is asked as follows: *"**How** do you mean?"* which has a number of benefits for us.

The first benefit is that we often get immediate clarification on the meaning of the communication (for example a statement or question) raised by the other person and very often they answer their own question once they've reflected on it.

This happens because asking 'How' causes a person to go internally to reflect and reframe their original question or statement so that it has a greater clarity for the listener (us).

They then re-state the question to us in the new format (or frame) making it clearer for us to understand.

The other benefit is that while they are re-considering their own question, we have more time to consider *our* response.

It's worth noting that the question "How do you mean?" is actually grammatically incorrect.

The more usual form of such a question is "**What** do you mean", which requests a much more specific answer. However, if you ask someone "**what** do they mean?' it is likely they will just say exactly what they just said and not take the time to explain it or reframe what they originally said.

It is the asking of "**How**" that causes the other person to go internally and reframe and re-consider their initial question or statement.

4. Answer-Assist Question

What happens when someone says, "I don't know" in answer to one of our questions? Often it tends to end a conversation and we have to find another way to raise the subject.

People usually answer "I don't know" to a question for three different reasons:

1. They have an answer but are concerned that they might be criticised or ridiculed when they give the answer and so they keep it to themselves.

2. They genuinely don't know the answer.

3. They don't wish to give an answer because they are trying to block further discussion on that subject as they may have an alternate agenda to ours.

Our response to an "I don't know" answer is therefore to break it into 3 distinct phases.

1. **Affirm**: tell them it's OK not to know the answer as this then relaxes them and lowers any tension.
2. **Delete**: now remove the fact that's it OK not to know the answer by using the word "But" (which usually deletes the meaning of whatever is said before this word is ever used).
3. **Request**: ask them to share in a non-threatening way.

Therefore, our response to an "I don't know" would sound something like this:

"I completely understand how you might not know at the moment BUT **if you <u>were</u> to know or just <u>suppose</u> you knew** *what would you say or what would you do?"*

The key here is *"<u>if</u>* **you were to know or just *suppose* you knew".**

This takes the person out of their current limited perception of the problem and allows them to search their full internal resources to come up with a solution.

Most people have understanding and knowledge available to them far beyond what they may be consciously aware of but most of this is stored at a deep and unconscious level.

By asking the question "if you were to know" or "just suppose you knew" or if "you could imagine a solution, what might that be" we give them permission to access that unconscious information from where it is stored in the brain and most importantly, we are not implying any negative judgement on their response. As a result, we remove any sense of threat on behalf of the other person.

At this point a person who had some uncertainty or hesitation about sharing their thoughts will usually share it with us as the question has removed any sense of negative criticism or judgement being made on their answer.

This is exactly what we want because the person is fully engaged and we can use their answer in some way that creates a collaborative solution to the question, ensuring a co-created and co-owned solution. Not something they are likely to easily or willingly walk away from.

In the case of a person who has no response because they still genuinely don't have an answer or continues to block us by again answering "I don't know" then we continue to move the process forward by taking control and saying:

'In that case ...may I make a suggestion...?'

The person who is genuinely stuck will gratefully accept the suggestion to allow us to move forward while the person who is attempting to block us must either accept the suggestion or reveal their reasons why they are not willing to engage on the topic with us.

5. Internal Representation Question

An internal representation question allows you to influence the mood (or state) someone is in.

People *literally* see the world differently when they are experiencing different feelings (bad or good) so we want them in the most positive mood possible when dealing with us.

For example, we might want a client or a colleague to associate a positive feeling with our service or product or project so we might ask – *"Can you remember a time...a specific time...*when you bought/experienced/were part of something you were really happy with, something that really pleased you, can you remember that time, a specific time?"

This causes them to associate back to that positive experience, re-establishing that good feeling and as we see them begin to smile and their physiology or body language shift (as it will) we then ask and "wouldn't it be great to feel that way again and this could just do that for you couldn't it?" (Note the tag question).

Don't you think we just might have their attention? It's just possible that we have that positive, receptive, feeling that all professionals know is the right mood for making a decision?

Equally we could also use it in a situation where we wanted to create a positive response from people to us personally.

Can you remember a time when you felt absolutely relaxed and confident with someone? A time when you knew you were learning from a real professional and you could see and feel all the benefits that would come from the learning, can you remember a specific time – now? And wouldn't it be nice to feel that way again? It would, wouldn't it?

A highly trusted advisor understands the power of being able to affect the emotional state of the other person and the impact they can create by heightening a person's emotional responses and thus influence their conscious decisions.

Listening Skills

Another key element in influencing others and ensuring that we are always 'in the room' when a person is speaking is being able to actively listen to their responses.

People that we engage with through effective questions and quality listening always engage more willingly and create faster rapport with us.

The following six steps outline some of the things to be aware of when conducting meetings and will immediately help to improve the quality of those meetings.

L stands for LOOK and Look Interested:

When in a meeting it is important that we maintain good eye contact with the other person at all times. Good eye contact indicates that we are expressing an interest in them and in his or her concerns.

Poor eye contact stems from not focusing our attention on the person's face or perhaps staring *too* intently at their features! There is a fine line between paying close and interested attention and seeming confrontational.

Looking at the person's face also allows us to pick up the unconscious facial signals that indicate the person's interest or lack of interest in what we are saying.

If for example, we notice that their eyes are going out of focus, we can safely assume that they are losing interest so we may require greater flexibility in our means of communication with them. Less talking and more questions perhaps? How about sketching it out on paper, getting them more involved in the meeting?

Some people prefer verbal communication while others prefer engaging through written communication. By bringing both into your presentation or meeting you can capture the full attention of anybody.

For those of us uncomfortable with eye contact (and many of us are) it's useful to remember to use what is known as the 'business triangle of vision' that we covered in an earlier chapter.

This inverted triangular space extends from across the eyebrows down to the tip of the chin.

When we direct our attention anywhere inside this area, we make the other person feel that we are completely engaging with them while removing the discomfort we might feel by focusing our attention on their eyeballs!

An additional benefit of being able to look at the person directly and having them feel really engaged with us is the fact that when we feel more comfortable with the communication, so do they.

In addition, many of us have a tendency to bring our mobile or cell phones with us to meetings and often unconsciously leave them on the table during a meeting.

What is the unconscious message that we are communicating to the other person? Are we saying that there is someone more important than them and we are just waiting for their call? Or are we clearly indicating that when we silence our phone and put it away, that I am entirely here, just for you.

I stands for IDENTIFY the Issues:

People are interested in what interests them, so find out what that is. The best means of doing that is to ask a very simple question – *"what's MOST important to you about...?"*

This question helps us to identify the values upon which a person makes their decisions. Usually, we would want to identify at least 3-4 values, and then identify the order in which they are most important.

Values are an important part of how people make their decisions. By identifying what they are we are better positioned to influence those same decisions.

Finding out what issues most concern the other person is a guaranteed way of gaining their interest and their attention and how we (or our services or leadership suggestions) can resolve their needs and wants for them.

S stands for SINCERITY:

We usually know when someone is being insincere with us. Is it something that's bound to win our trust? So why would the people whom we want to influence be any different?
Never promise things we can't deliver on. Always deliver a little more than is expected. Respect other people as we would ourselves and ensure that above all else, our dealings with others are based on the highest sense of integrity.

Relationships built on sincerity and integrity will last. It is on these relationships that our business and career future is secured.

T stands for TEST Your Understanding of what the other person is saying:

Too often we can make errors in our suggestions, because we failed to question a person sufficiently around the specifics of their needs or because we made an assumption.

It's OK to ask questions for clarification around what another person is most concerned about but it's not OK to *assume* we know their needs, as every person is different.

After all, as a sales professional or leader we want to provide the best solution possible, don't we? The best way of doing that is to question for a clearer understanding of the needs of each person in turn.

A simple question that one can ask when seeking clarification is the Exploratory or "How do you mean?" question or "what *specifically...*" This question encourages the person to reflect on their statement and then repeat it back to us in a more coherent way often allowing them to furnish us with information that may have been left out of the earlier answer.

E stands for ENTHUSIASM:

There is no substitute for being sincerely enthusiastic about providing a solution to a client or stakeholder's needs.

No matter how experienced we might be in business, enthusiasm, that expression of a 'can do' attitude when meeting with the client or colleague, has a magical effect.

Enthusiasm is infectious. It portrays a willingness to serve and to do our best in the process. It is an excellent influencing tool in the process of reaching agreement with others. In a business development or leadership role it is invaluable.

It's also worth noting that the last four letters of Enthusiasm – I.A.S.M – stand for *'I Am Sold Myself!'* If we bring what we love to our prospects, clients, colleagues, team members and stakeholders how hard can it be to get them to love it too?

N stands for NODS, NOISES and NOTES:

By feeding back to a person our understanding, agreement and interest to what they are saying through unconscious body language such as short verbal comments and nods, we communicate to them that we are pacing their conversation and are maintaining interest in what concerns them.

By communicating only through nods and noises we are acknowledging them, giving them permission and encouraging them to keep talking thus gathering further information around a specific topic until it's time for us to again control the conversation through asking a relevant question.

Notes are invaluable in meetings. Do not expect to remember it all.

Do try to take any notes discreetly, keeping them short to ensure we maintain maximum eye contact and direct interaction with the person and remember that it is polite to ask if it's OK to take notes during the meeting before you start to write.

However, not only is it polite but when you do ask permission to take notes at the start of your meeting, then while you are taking notes the other person will keep their attention and eye contact focused on you while you do so. This removes the need to rebuild engagement each time you take a note because you have broken eye contact.

So next time you are meeting with a client, colleague or stakeholder, remember the influence value in having the other person do most of the talking.

9

Learning to Love Objections

Objections are normal in business communications, whether made to a sales proposal or when presenting a project for approval to colleagues or other internal stakeholders so now let's explore why we as advisors should *actively seek them out* rather than avoid them.

One of the greatest concerns that all professionals have is being able to deal with and positively influence objections to their business proposals. The following points can help us to see how valuable and necessary having to face and handle objections to our proposals are in the business process.

Objections can act as guides as to how far along the process of successfully influencing others we are, how good we are communicating our intentions, how well we are doing with getting agreement from a prospect or how close we are to closing the project proposal with a key stakeholder.

Objections occur for any number of reasons. Perhaps we haven't been listening actively for example and so missed a key piece of information or failed to ask the right kind of question to clarify a person's response. Or perhaps we have not addressed the objection sufficiently and there is a significant degree of ambiguity or lack of clarity in the mind of the other person.

We might even be attempting to communicate our information in a way that is the complete opposite of the other person's preferred style of communication. (See the earlier chapter on Connecting in Colour).

Personally, when objections are genuine (and not just being used to block or impede the presentation or to make the person look good to his/her peers), I *love* to get objections to my proposals and there are a number of reasons why:

1. We Often Confuse an 'Objection' With a 'Rejection'.

One of my father's favourite sayings is *"It's nothing personal, just business."*

Well business objections is just that; not personal, just business.

Remember that a person is not rejecting **us** they are objecting to our **business proposition**. In the case of a sales prospect they often do not even **know** us, in fact, they may know little or nothing about us personally so how can they be rejecting *us?*

What they are *really* objecting to is the lack of understanding or clarity that they have about how the product, service or the project that we are proposing brings any value or benefit to them.

What they're really saying is that they want more information, before they can make a decision.

2. In Business "No" Seldom Means "No – For Forever" Just "No - For Now".

Many professionals often give up on a presentation or a proposal when the decision-maker first says "No".

But I'm going to ask you *not to stop* at the first "No" you get. When a person says "No" they often have some deeper reason below it and so what we really need to do is to probe deeper into the real reason for the "No".

By doing so we may discover that the timing is not right, or they are not the right decision maker, or that we don't have the right service offering or project for them, or they may not have the budgets or just that they may not understand what we're actually proposing (poorly communicated).

Find out *why* they said "No" in the first place and it may allow us to position the business proposition again at a later date in a more pertinent way. To do this a really well-formed question that can help us with this challenge is to ask: *"May I ask, why specifically, on this occasion you are saying "no"?"* – and that will help us identify the *real* objection. Never be afraid to ask the other person to justify their objection or push back at them gently. It may just help us to find out the real motivation and then adapt us to adapt our presentation accordingly.

3. Objections are Better than Indifference.

I can work with an objection because I can probe it or I can change the way I'm communicating. If they're objecting to what I'm presenting, then at least *they are still engaged in the process* and trying to understand what it is we are proposing.

They are looking for more information or clarity or a reason to buy or support a proposal.

What I can't and won't attempt to influence or persuade is someone who is *indifferent*, where they demonstrate that have obviously zero interest in what I'm proposing and may even be displaying passive aggressive behaviour.

This can only occur if we've gotten our prospecting criteria wrong in the first place and we are talking to the wrong business stakeholder. Alternatively, it may happen because we have committed some error that we are not aware of that has caused them some degree of annoyance, or has broken rapport and hence created passive resistance to us or the proposal.

Either way, it's time to move on. 'Pitching' an idea, product or service is about demonstrating how we can bring value to the other person, never about trying to push what we have. The world is an abundant place and it's so much easier to work with people who have a need for our products, services or our ideas. Retreat, regroup and retarget and find the people who want to work with us.

4. Maybe We're Not Communicating in *Their* Language.

Different people communicate and process information in different ways. (Chapter 9 Connecting in Colour).

Some are '*Visual*' so they like pictures and graphs (Red Warriors). They process information through pictures so they need to see brochures or graphs or models.

Some people are *'Auditory'* (Yellow Influencers) or do their mental processing through sound. As a result, they like to talk and verbalise things with others and require personal interaction and the chance to vocalise.

Other prospects are *'Feeling'* (Green Healers) and like time to reflect and 'get a feel' for the product, service or proposal. They might want to handle, touch the product or be assured that others are already using a service successfully and speak well of it.

Finally, some people are *'Analytical'* (Blue Scholars) and prefer to get their information in written form in advance of any sales pitch or project meeting so that they have the time to reflect on and analyse the proposition and do not want to be forced into making a decision.

Just as an small example I once consulted with a software company in Dallas, Texas who had a problem with the ratio of the number of personal appointments they were getting compared to the number of phone calls they were making to get an appointment.

By just taking the time to learn about the personality types (colour preferences) that their sales team sold to (bankers – predominantly Blue) and the personality style of their sales team (predominantly Red-Yellow), they learned to move from an visual/auditory style to an reflective/analytical style and so increase their call to appointment ratio by almost a factor of ten.

They actually increased their 'call to meeting' ratio from just 4 appointments in every 100 calls to 38 appointments in every 100 calls. Now that's progress.

To be sure that we get our point across effectively we must make sure that we **use verbal, visual and written styles** to make the most effective presentation.

5. Handle Objections with 'Specifically'

Ambiguity or a lack of clarity can kill a business or project proposal so we need to ensure that we get the *facts* and not general responses or assumptions.

If a person makes a generalised statement or creates an objection we can often get a great deal of clarity around it and handle it successfully if we probe using the six 'open' questions (How, What, Where, Why, When and Who) and use the word **Specifically**.

How **Specifically**, When **Specifically**, Who **Specifically** and so on can have the prospect or stakeholder review their objections and allow us to find a way through the objection and carry on with the business process.

6. Each Objection is a Step Closer to the Prize

Every objection successfully met and dealt with is a step closer to getting your desired outcome from a meeting - whether that is a sale to a client or maybe the acceptance of feedback by a team member. Not only that but objections can be turned around and turned into reasons to act.

"You don't have it in blue" – "If I could get it for you in blue would you be interested in going ahead?"

"I don't have the budget" – "If we could bill you in the *next* quarter could we then look at proceeding?"

"it's too expensive" – "May I ask compared to who? Maybe we could tailor it closer to your budget by removing some elements of the proposal?"

Objections can be a tremendous help in calibrating where we are in the meeting process.

Because questions can indicate that the other person is engaging with us and exhibiting a degree of interest they are far better than having to handle indifference.

Each objection successfully handled is a step closer to closing the deal or getting support for a project so do learn to welcome them and use them as valuable tools in creating even greater personal rapport and business success by sustaining and monetising the lifetime value of the client or by winning over more company stakeholders to our proposals and projects.

In the next chapter we explore a key skill for any influencer, delivering winning presentations.

10

Tips for More Successful Presentations

A critical skill for anyone who wants to be a highly trusted advisor and communicator is being able to successfully present our solution, service or project proposal or an 'all hands' or conference speech.

Finally, the time to pitch our idea, our project or business message has arrived and here is where we can either fail disastrously or emerge victorious from the time and effort we have invested in initiating, nurturing and deepening our relationship with the prospect, client or key company stakeholder or audience.

Even if the audience is one of existing clients or colleagues (perhaps key business stakeholders or staff) how competent we are seen to be as a presenter or speaker can hugely impact on our professional brand.

In this chapter I want to highlight some key factors that can enhance the power of our presentations and the value of the 'take aways' that an audience gets from our presentations.

The quality and number of these key learning points will ensure that our presentation is both memorable and successful.

1. The **WHW** Structure:

Given the increased 'distraction' spans of modern audiences, the structure of a presentation is even more critical than ever. It is the one area where presentations can go badly wrong right from the start.

We live in a world where the attention span of an audience competes with ever more 'instruments of mass distraction' and therefore is restricted to those things that grab their interest from the start.

An audience's attention can be won or lost in the first few minutes of the presentation, so we need to capture their attention right from the very start.

However, despite this I still see presentations that start with the old traditional approach of *Who* we are (lots of information about our company, our team or ourselves that nobody really cares about anymore). *How* we are so great at what we do and *What* (finally!) we can do for you. It's all about the company and not focused on the audience's needs and wants.

It is an information pitch (about us) and not a value pitch (all about the benefits and value to them). The result of this traditional presentation structure (especially with Red Warrior decision-makers) is an immediate loss of attention. The audience has already tuned-out by the time you get to the value proposition and so decision-makers are no longer engaged.

This traditional presentation structure needs to be *inverted* or turned on its head and away from the traditional Who, How and What to **What, How and Who/Why** instead.

We should *start* our presentation by leading with the **WHAT** *we can do for you* or WHAT we value or benefits we intend to give you. Here is where we clearly state right from the start the value benefits that we can bring to the audience and therefore their reward for paying attention and listening to our presentation. Always position the value to the audience right from the start.

State clearly and distinctly for the audience what *specifically* they will get when they work with or support us (and here's a chance to use our 'Points of Compelling Relevance/Engagement') so that the language is simple, concise, meaningful and present tense.

In addition, if we have done our research correctly, we can place each PCR against a specific client or stakeholder value that we have identified and sequenced in earlier meetings using our questioning skills.

Think what a powerful impact that can make.

Once we have captured the audiences' attention by starting with the value and benefits (in clear simple language) that they will get from using our services or products or supporting our projects (and we have aligned those benefits with their key decision-making values) the audience automatically then wants an answer to the next question that they are already thinking.

Now the question in the audience's mind is **How** can we deliver this? They are interested, engaged and seeking answers. They *want* to know, so we continue to hold their engagement.

So instead of their attention having been lost from the start they are actively listening, filling in the blanks, searching for ways in which their issues can be resolved. They are with us on the journey.

Finally, the audience will ask **Who We Are or Why** they should work with us and at this point is where we establish our credibility, experience and resources. This is the final piece of the journey that the audience has willingly taken with us and where they are now convinced of the value of our proposal.

So, I suggest that we move from the traditional structure of Why, How and What to the more effective and engaging structure of **What, How and Who/Why** and see the impact of our presentations soar.

I regularly coach professionals and business-owners to professional speaker standards and part of that is for them to stop thinking about presentations in the traditional formal manner. Audiences want to be connected, understood, involved and engaged so think about how we structure a *dialogue* or conversation with the audience and not just a *monologue* or a presentation.

Professional speakers focus on having a *conversation* (or even *a facilitation)* with the audience but no longer a formal *presentation*. Here's some of the ways that they start to do that in a presentation or speech.

1 . They Start a Presentation With and Use Stories Throughout.

Remember as a child the power of the words "Once Upon a Time"?

It instantly prepared us for story time, for adventures and magic and tales of faraway places and mythical lands dropping us into a powerfully suggestible trance. Stories are how humanity has shared information and experience from the very first of days. Notice the longevity of mythological stories and how even today we perk up when someone has news or a bit of gossip. It's how we forge tribes and a powerful way to create inclusion and bring the audience into our presentation.

Stories in presentations are thus very powerful and we should craft stories that can serve as metaphors or platforms for our key business points.

Some reasons for why stories are powerful presentation tools are as follows:

1. There is little resistance to stories as people do not see themselves as being 'pitched at' or 'sold to' when stories are used to illustrate points, so their normal resistance and scepticism is lowered.

2. The audience associates with the characters in a story, mentally and emotionally taking the position and the viewpoint of the key person and living their experiences in the story. This can be a powerful suggestive tool encouraging people to take the same decisions or actions as the story's central character.

3. Stories don't have to be true they just have to be *plausible*. Stories do not have to be dry, cold case studies and so they can be powerful means of suggesting things to an audience.

   Also, because they are stories, we can use them to position ideas in the mind of an audience without the necessity for exact logical proof. Simply being plausible, that something is possible, is often enough to get the message across and effect change in the mind of the audience.

4. Developing stories, either real case studies but converted into genuine stories rather than cold facts or with stories that are simply created to highlight a key point, allows us to powerfully influence any audience. We can turn any 'cold' case study into a 'warm' story by simply given names to the people in the study.

2 . They Develop Self-Confidence:

Presenting to a live audience for some people is sometimes a greater fear than even death or injury. People will literally do anything to get out of having to make a presentation to a group.

I have personally seen how this fear can paralyse and render incapable otherwise very intelligent and articulate people. Managing one's confidence is therefore important if one wishes to appear fluent, competent and professional.

First, let me just say that it's OK to be nervous. In fact, it's a *good thing* because it means that we genuinely *care* about the presentation and our message.

Someone once *said; "it's perfectly OK to have butterflies in your stomach as long as they are all flying in formation!"* Personally, I always get nervous before a speech or presentation and I use those nerves to help keep me sharp.

In fact, I'd be worried if I wasn't nervous because it could mean that I am not concerned enough about how the presentation might go and that's just not acceptable for me as it would impact on me giving my full potential to the audience. So, nerves can actually *help* a presenter or speaker to sharpen their focus and delivery.

However *too* many nerves are not good and so we need to learn to manage our state and confidence prior to any presentation. So here are a few pointers that may help:

1. Live Rehearsal - helps fluency and (very importantly) timing. (By the way always finish a presentation on time. Two minutes before time and they love us, two minutes after the time and they are looking for a way out of the room).
Repetition is internalisation, so the more often we do it in rehearsal the more likely it is to be successful in real life. As they say in martial arts (an interest of mine), the more you sweat in training, the less you bleed in battle.
Deliver your presentation out loud, walk around as if you are doing the presentation, practice with your deck and slide clicker. Rehearse however and wherever you can. Then when it comes to doing it for real you will have done it so often you will have created the presentation equivalent of 'muscle memory', it just flows automatically because you've already delivered it a hundred times before the event.

2. Mental Rehearsal – repeatedly rehearsing an imagined successful outcome to your presentation over and over in our mind is a powerful means of managing personal state and is used extensively by professional athletes.

From psychology we know that the mind cannot tell the difference between a real and imagined memory so the more often we rehearse things in our mind the more the mind believes that this is something that we do every day so what are we nervous for?

Picture the audience being interested, engaged and giving us a powerfully positive reception to our presentation. This helps reduce the fear of the event because the mind assumes that this is a familiar thing for us and not something being done for the first time.

3 . Put something relevant about ourselves into the opening of a presentation.

At the very start of the presentation, where it is appropriate, we should take the opportunity to introduce ourselves with something that connects us with the audience.

There are two benefits to this:

1. It allows us to talk about the one thing that no-one can question us on, ourselves.
   We are the expert about ourselves and this can help us start to relax into the presentation as we talk about a subject that we are completely knowledgeable on.

2. It also allows us to start to build a relationship with the audience by sharing something in our introduction that connects with them or their interests.

4 . Finally, always remember your authority as an expert.

We are in the room with the audience's expectation that we are already an expert in the subject of our presentation. If we have rehearsed and prepared then there is no reason why we cannot deliver on that expectation every time.

When it comes to confidence in a presentation the difference between fear and fluency is passion and practice.

Engaging the Audience

Managing an audience is critical to a successful presentation. So, let's look at a few pointers that can help with this area too.

1 . The Light House:

Keeping an audience's attention involves maintaining good eye contact. That means that we need to 'sweep' the audience with our eyes on a regular basis just like a lighthouse. This ensures that the audience sees that we are engaged, that we continue to assess audience reactions and it helps keep the audience itself on their toes and awake!

This is particularly important when we are using a slide presentation or a flipchart.

There can be a tendency to read the screen or turn away from the audience and that can be disastrous because breaking eye contact with an audience can cause us to lose their attention.

To minimise this happening, we should have a copy of the presentation in front of us, where we can glance at it without having to turn away from the audience. Sometimes it's possible to have another screen positioned in front of us that matches what is being shown on the main screen.

2 . Use Questions:

We have already looked in detail in a previous chapter at the power of questions and suggestions and the advanced questioning skills that we can bring to bear on a prospect or client or colleague, as a means of managing a meeting.

But questions can also be used in presentations to ensure that the audience is fully engaged in the presentation. In the modern world (depending on the size of the audience) we are moving away from direct 'presentations' to more group 'facilitations' and questions are a critical tool for that.

As I said at the start of this chapter, modern presentations (particularly in this hybrid age) need to be less about us having a monologue (one-way communication) with the audience and more about a dialogue (two-way communication) that is so much more powerful and engaging?

The challenge can sometimes be in competently handling questions from the audience however and so here are a couple of ideas about how handle them professionally and fluently.

A. The Car Park:

Sometimes time constraints on a presentation can reduce the time to adequately deal with questions. One way to ensure that we have the time to complete our presentation and deal with any and all questions is to use what's called the Car Park.

Agree with the audience from the start that to ensure that we finish on time, that we will not answer their questions during the presentation. However, we will happily take questions from the floor as they arise and note them on a flip-chart.

Once we have delivered the presentation then the last thing that we do is then turn to the flip-chart where we have written down the audience's questions.

As we move down the list of questions, answering each one of them in turn, we will find that a number of the questions have already been dealt with during the presentation. Other questions will not have been dealt with and so we use the opportunity now to answer those questions.

As we answer each question, use a marker to place a big 'tick' or 'correct' sign beside each answered question.

By leaving this on display, when we bring the session to an end the audience (as they depart) can see that every question has been answered and every question is 'correct' and has been resolved. This can be a powerful visual anchor for an audience to have at the end of any presentation.

B. Handling Difficult Questions

When faced with difficult questions from the audience how we handle them will be a clear indicator as to our professionalism as an advisor and communicator.

First, if we do not know the answer to the question *then say so* but we can then use it as an opportunity to compliment then questioner.

We might say something like: *"That is an excellent question. To be honest I had not considered it but if you are happy to give me a little time, I'll come back to you with the relevant answer if I may?"*

Then make sure that we do (with supporting documentation) and ensure that the rest of the audience knows that we have. Copy them for example on the email that responds to the question.

Secondly, a question can sometimes be asked because the questioner wishes to assert their dominance in the group or their knowledge or to get attention or simply to throw us off balance.

In such a case we can often throw a difficult question back at someone or have them justify or clarify the question by saying *"Interesting question. You seem to have given this some thought so may I ask, what are your own thoughts?"*

Alternatively, if the person has been consistently interrupting a presentation to score points or gain attention then we might ask them a difficult question and before they have time to respond say *"and while X are considering that let us move on with the presentation and we can then come back.".*

A variation on that is to ask the rest of the audience to comment with *"that is an interesting perspective. May I ask what the rest of the audience think?"* I've seen this question used to powerful effect on an audience. When asked, the audience themselves then challenged the questioner and made their opinion felt as to what they thought about the constant interruption.

It is very important that we as the presenter avoid engaging in argument with a member of the audience. Doing so can only lose us key credibility and rapport with an audience.

While we cannot cover every aspect of the psychology of presentations or keynoting and conference speaking here, these simple pointers can help add a professional, confident and effective edge to any presentation we make and ensure that our presentations are more memorable, engaging and successful.

11

The Psychology of Performance Goals

Success is often defined as the *achievement of pre-defined goals*.

Therefore, to be successful requires that we have clear written goals that map out our desires and the actions necessary to take them.

More importantly, well-defined and articulated goals are powerful tools when a highly trusted advisor works in a coaching style with team members or colleagues. If we can help others identify, define, articulate and break down their objectives then we can powerfully support their achievement of these goals through measurement and shared ownership and accountability.

In the next two chapters I'll cover the psychology behind setting goals that work. We'll look at some of the key secrets of setting and achieving powerful new outcomes and we'll also cover the ways to make goal-setting a fantastic habit for mega-success and how it can boost our motivation to keep us and our teams or colleagues going when others surrender.

Nothing great was ever achieved without planning.

Many successful businesses lay plans for the future, yet it constantly amazes me how few of the people charged with delivering business goals have actually set specific goals for their own personal performance. This is where engaging an executive or business coach can add huge value to a career or a business.

Taking the time to understand clearly how to set and achieve goals can provide us all with 7 key benefits:

1. A clear direction in our lives and profession and a sense of adventure about its outcome.

2. A measure by which to benchmark the successes that we have along the way.

3. A boost in our self-confidence, as a result of our success and enhanced sense of control.

4. A powerful means of coping with change and stress. By knowing in advance what we can do to adapt and succeed despite the challenges that we face, we can cope with the stress of future uncertainty more effectively.

5. The ability to communicate our needs more effectively. Once we know clearly what we want and why we want it, then enlisting the aid of others through communicating our intention improves our success rate and again reduces our personal stress levels and maximises our performance.

6. The ability to improve our strengths and overcome our weaknesses. Often by identifying our strengths and working towards them, we overcome our weaknesses by removing their impact as they become less relevant because of the actions that we take to move forward.

7. A better quality (and balance) of work and life. This can be assisted by all of the above benefits of deciding what the future *should* be instead of waiting for what life will throw at you. It is better to create one's future than it is to try and predict it.

Yet despite these obvious benefits, many professionals still do one thing wonderfully well, we take the time to plan to fail, simply by failing to plan.

Check yourself against these reasons of why we people often fail to plan our future success:

1. We don't understand the importance of setting goals.
2. We fear failure and/or rejection.
3. We fear success.
4. We simply don't take the time.
5. We don't know how to set goals or set them too high initially and get discouraged from further action.
6. We fail to raise our personal standards.
7. We fail to empower our goals by using our subconscious mind and understanding our motivation.

Let's look at some of the main reasons of why we still fail to set specific outcomes for ourselves:

We Fear Failure/Rejection: We can consider both of these together because fear of failure is often closely linked to the fear of rejection.

Acceptance is the highest of human needs as we are essentially social creatures and so anything that threatens that need for acceptance is to be instinctively avoided. However, if in protecting our sense of ourselves, we let that same sense wither and die for want of taking a risk, where is the excitement in life's game?

Even failure is a process of learning. Every time we fail, we learn the next time to use a different approach. Our brains are wired to do this. For those of us who can swim we had to swallow a lot of water before we achieved proficiency. Every time we sank our instinctive learning mechanism filed away the learning by which we could do it better the next time.

In the same way we learned to ride a bicycle by failing and by taking the learning from the failure until we built up a sufficient understanding of the process to do it right and then improve upon it. Our brain analysed our failures, converted them into learnings and applied them until we had 'hard wired' the new behaviours into our system creating a habit or a competency.

Success is often a gradual process. Few if any 'overnight' successes have no history of failures from which years later their 'overnight' success was born.

We should 'dare to fail' and in the failing, find the learning that leads to a better understanding of the means of achieving our goal. Few rewards are earned without risk and those that are we seldom value.

Successful people know that life and business are not about being 'perfect' but about 'perfecting' where the journey requires us to fail, to learn from it, to be human, to forgive and to grow.

We Fear Success: It's strange to consider that we might actually fear success. But in fact, this is one of our greatest fears.

This is because success brings responsibility. It creates standards that once we create them, we have to continue to live up to. Standards that then can be used to criticise us should we fail at some future, undefined date, to meet them.

It also brings a fear of the consequences that may occur after we have achieved our desired goals. If I achieve this goal, what would I lose? Who would I upset? Have you ever heard someone say, "I'd LOVE to win a few million in the Lottery, you know three or maybe four million...but NOT twenty million... no...that'd ruin your life!"

So, we sometimes need to check the possible consequences of achieving our goals. When setting a personal or professional goal it can be important to ask first 'what would I gain if I achieve this goal?' or 'what would I lose if I gain this goal?'

If the answer is in conflict with either our personal or professional values, then the chances are that we could have a significant lack of motivation towards achieving this goal.

We Don't Take the Time: We can always find the time for what we really consider as important can't we? Deciding on goals is an unconscious process, something we do quite naturally every day. What makes the *difference* in our performance is when we prioritise, clarify and commit them to paper or interactive PDF.

The relatively little time taken to invest in setting down goals can lead to far greater rewards, from far less effort. Self-discipline is the key. Make a start. Then it becomes surprisingly easy and even fun.

Alternatively find a successful coach to work with (ahem!) someone who will help you define those new horizons or performance goals and work with you until you have reached them, usually faster than you would do on your own.

We Don't Know How to Set Goals Properly: In the first flush of each New Year, we often set resolutions that last as long as the month of January.

We often we set our resolutions (or goals) too high, setting ourselves up for failure through overreaching ourselves. This then often discourages us from further endeavours. That's understandable, for when were we ever shown how to create a manual for our life or our career?

Perhaps we may have had to struggle through some of our life or career up to now. But now we have the power to change that, now we have the power to choose our destinies and make them real through focused action.

We Fail to Raise Our Personal or Professional Standards: As long as we expect little of ourselves, we will get just that - little. Our expectations drive our behaviours and those of others around us.

Our future should be dictated not by what has gone before but by the decisions that we make in the present. In deciding to create a new future, we first raise our standards and our expectations of ourselves and of those around us.

It is the nature of life that if we are not learning and growing, then we are stagnating. We get exactly what the mind expects. Positive thinking is thinking about what you want. Instead, most of us focus our minds on what we don't want. As a result, we get exactly what we *don't* want to happen.

Our expectations should always exceed our experiences.

Goals fill our 'neural network' with the programming necessary to create the desired behaviour for our success and expectations drive behaviours.

We Fail to Empower Goals with Our Subconscious or Our Emotions:
Our subconscious mind is a huge neural resource. Success is guaranteed when we learn to access it for our goals and begin the process of *synchronicity*.

Synchronicity is the means whereby we become aware of attracting people or things into our lives by deciding on a goal. It's almost as if we send out an unconscious signal that feeds back the information that we need to be successful in our efforts.

Focusing on something specific raises our awareness of possibilities and opens opportunities aligned with the object of our focus. As a simple example, have you ever considered buying a car and then when you paid for it (invested value in it) *that* was when you noticed just how many of that particular type of car there are actually on the roads, you just never noticed before, until you *focused* on it.

Now having considered the importance of our goals, let's consider the foundations of how power-goals are formed and mega-achievement created.

There are 5 foundations to achievable outcomes or successful goals.

The first is **VISION**.

Vision is the capacity to see beyond where we are in the present and imagine a future that is all that it can be. This *encourages* us to raise our standards and gives us the capability to start to overcome the self-limiting beliefs that are often part of our programming as children.

We can often obstruct this creative faculty within us. We are conditioned to believe that all the goals we set should be realistic and achievable.

While most goals certainly need to be achievable to maintain our motivation, when *all* our goals are based entirely on our experiences and beliefs about ourselves to-date, our ability to leap to a new plateau of performance is greatly limited. Sometimes it pays to "take the road less travelled".

The great leaders through history, all of them visionaries willing to look beyond the boundaries of convention, have always been inspired by visions of greater glories or worlds that have yet to be. For good or ill it is precisely because of those visions that the world progressed.

Inspiration is motivation.

The second is **DESIRE**.

A want is stronger than a wish. We often achieve what we want but seldom what we wish for. Desire is born when we associate more pleasure than pain with the outcome. Therefore, we should set goals only for what we really desire.

Only goals that are meaningful to us will be fuelled by the power of desire. Desire is the inner fire that sets our futures alight.

Setting goals simply because they appear impressive to others wastes our time. Setting goals because they return a real and tangible benefit for us creates the motivation we need to move toward our specified outcomes.

The third foundation is **RESPONSIBILITY**.

Responsibility is essential to success.

It is essential to achieving our outcomes in the fast moving and digital/AI world of today and tomorrow. We must hold ourselves accountable for our actions and decisions.

Reaching for goals involves challenge. By taking responsibility for the way in which we meet those challenges, by being honest with ourselves, we can apply the flexibility necessary to meet those challenges and achieve our objectives.

The secret to having more control over our careers and lives is simple.

TAKE MORE RESPONSIBILITY.

The fourth is **COMMITMENT**.

Goals without personal commitment are just wasted effort.

We must begin a thing and learn to accept our failures, for failures there may be, as *learning* rather than as setbacks.

Our level of commitment is determined by the amount of gain or pleasure we subscribe to the achievement of our goals. Commitment also means that we take those first steps to achievement, which can often prove the hardest.

But to overcome the inertia that is at first associated with great undertakings - *simply begin.*

In time, if we have set our goals correctly, the successes of the smaller goals will drive us forward to successfully reach our overall outcome. Commitment requires the steel of self-discipline and the ability to see our focus and our desires through to their fulfilment.

The fifth foundation is **HONEST EVALUATION**.

There's a saying that says that "you can lie to everybody else, but always be true to yourself."

We must be prepared to tell ourselves the 'hard stuff' about whether we are really putting in the effort to make things happen. We need to monitor ourselves regularly about our level of commitment and the tasks achieved to-date.

This has the added bonus of improving our flexibility to decide new plans of action where circumstances merit, making sure that we stay on track, until we reach our goal. The most important thing about goals is the ability to make them a part of our everyday thinking. Make them a habit for ourselves so that *every day* we take action towards their achievement and our satisfaction.

One of the ways of creating a habit or *an unconscious repetitive response* is to create goals in a manner that they are easily accepted by the powerhouse of our Unconscious mind.

Our Unconscious (or Subconscious) mind has a number of important points about which all successful coaches, mentors, leaders and advisors should be aware.

1. The Unconscious mind is designed to protect and heal the body.

The unconscious mind's prime directive is to protect and heal the body, even if that means making us sick sometimes. For example, if excessive stress is wearing us down, the Unconscious can make us sick in order to take the rest that the body needs.

Take athletes who are coping badly with the pressure of an important game, it is amazing how many ankles get sprained, or illnesses set-in prior to the game. Take a performer or someone who develops stage fright, how many develop laryngitis or tonsillitis before a show. In this case, for our unconscious mind, physical illness is better than facing the fear of what they are expected to do.

As a result, successful planning should take into consideration both our professional and personal agendas in order to ensure that balance and harmony is maintained and that we can enjoy the fruits of our achievement.

There should be an ecological side to our planning, not in the sense of the natural environment of the planet, but in an understanding of the *consequences* of the goals we set.

2. The mind loves priority, association and specificity.

The mind reacts better when things have a sense of urgency about them and so goals should be prioritised in order of importance, first things first.

It also loves association or linkages so ideally similar or supporting goals should be grouped together. This helps our unconscious focus more effectively on them. It encourages further links between the goals as the creative and intuitive side of the unconscious goes to work on making life that much easier for itself, by often providing unique new ways to achieve goals.

The unconscious mind is lazy and takes the easy way out wherever possible. Therefore, goals should be as specific as possible.

It's not enough to say I want 'more money' for walking down the street and finding a coin fulfils that requirement as far as the unconscious is concerned. Be specific, HOW MUCH MONEY SPECIFICALLY...do you want.

Make it work for you and never settle for less than that.

The remarkable thing about our mind is that it will move heaven and earth to ensure that what is happening in our *external* world, is a direct reflection of our *internal* world and our *internal* world is a direct reflection of the expectations that we create through setting power goals.

For example, can you remember how the world often seems a terrible place when things aren't going too well and yet how wonderful it appears and how lucky you seem to be when you're feeling GREAT!

As Professor Bruce Lipton says, "if you want to create heaven on earth simply fall in love". If you've ever fallen in love it's like the world changes overnight to being the most perfect place ever where everything is suddenly possible, everything is wonderful. Yet, nothing externally has really changed, just our perception of things based on the hormones running through our system. Hence the phrase, 'change your mind, change your life'.

Change your mind and you can change your world. When coaching top leaders and professionals I often remind them of the phrase 'that attitude is 80% of success'. In other words, what they expect is often what they will get.

Expectations drive behaviours.

3. The subconscious mind holds the majority of our mental energy.

The subconscious mind has long been likened to the 90% of iceberg that lies beneath the surface of the water. It is silent, deep and powerful. I also like to think it is more like the engine room of a ship. It doesn't see where the ship is bound, that's the job of the captain on the bridge (the conscious mind). But it provides the power to drive the ship across the wild and wide seas of life. The ship is powerless and directionless until the conscious and subconscious minds are working in harmony, direction and motivation.

4. It accepts simple, present tense, instructions.

The subconscious recognises no past or future. Only the present exists in its world.

Therefore, all instructions to it such as goals should be structured that way. After all, it drives our physical health and wellbeing. What if it instructed your heart to beat in thirty minutes time or that the next time you drew a breath would be next week?

How immediately and in what tense do you think it needs to receive its instructions about our *other* needs?

Write your goals using the five P's:

Positive such that the goal or need is stated in a positive sense.

Present Tense as explained above, so that it impacts more urgently on our Subconscious mind.

Personal again to help to drive the Unconscious which recognises only itself.

Passionate using emotive words to drive the Subconscious that responds to strong emotions.

Particular or exactly and specifically stated so that the unconscious knows exactly what it must do.

Our intention is very important when setting goals so to ensure the best results start your goals by writing "I want... or I am." That is a much more powerful statement of intent than I wish, I would, I hope etc. For example, "I am earning", "I am sleeping", I am living", "I am working" etc. or "I sleep", "I live", "I work" etc.

5. The Unconscious mind cannot tell the difference between real and imagined memories.

Can you remember a time when you recounted an event that had happened to you, only to make yourself look better or seem to have played a larger part in the event than actually occurred, let's say you embellished the story of the event *just a little* when re-telling the event later to some friends?

Then you told the story again and again and again and then you forgot about it, until someone asked you to tell the story but 6 months later. Only now you couldn't remember what had *actually* happened and what you had added, it was *all* real to you.

Repetition had created a reality composed of truth and half-truth.

When working with the unconscious mind things only have to be *plausible* to be accepted as fact. In effect, we can recreate our past histories leaving our failures behind and reprogramming only the experiences of success into our future behaviours.

Clinical hypnosis techniques make use of this fact when helping people safely revisit old and emotional memories and handle the emotions surrounding them.

A person can relive the event in a safe way, take the learning and shift the grief or fear associated with the event, which leads to a subsequent improvement in the person's behaviour and health.

6. It processes through vivid pictures and strong emotions - mental rehearsal.

Our unconscious neural network is programmed through clear, vivid pictures and with strong emotion.

That is why we must *create a vivid image* of our future goal and the more colourful the image the better. In fact, if we add *sound, movement, brightness, clarity, even smells* to the future picture, then the *more* real it becomes to our 'movie of the mind'.

Where possible we should include ourselves in some way in the picture we create. This communicates to our unconscious that *this* is its target.

If we experience the future as if we have it, the Unconscious assumes that we have achieved our goal already and will not focus on the objective. This is known as dissociated and associated mental rehearsal but more of this later.

Vivid emotion comes from the fact that our goal should be meaningful to us. The unconscious is the seat of our emotions and through them we can stimulate and communicate with it.

Whatever way you imagine the goal is perfectly OK as some people will be more colourful or accurate or clear than others, some people use 'story or vision boards' to help capture and hold the images they want.

In the Unconscious there is no such thing as doing it the wrong way once a positive intent or meaning is attached to the thought.

Within us all is the power to change worlds. It is in the imagination that the empires of the past were first raised and within the fires of the imagination that the dreams of the future are born.

Learning to use that imagination to empower your goals (and those of others) is a valuable skill for a leader, coach or advisor. The subconscious mind is the seat of our emotions and provides the desire and energy to motivate us to achieve our intended objectives.

We communicate with our unconscious through the use of vividly imagined scenarios or pictures and emotions. It is important that while we create these pictures in our mind, we also create the imagined sounds, tastes, smells, touches and feelings that would accompany the experience.

In effect, imagine that we can create a theatre in our mind and that we can create, as the director of our own movie of success any scene that we choose.

If we then invest that scene with the feelings, sounds, tastes, smells etc. we are, in effect, programming our mental computer to generate the behaviour that will lead us to our goal.

What we are doing through such programming is creating expectations, which in turn create new 'engrams' or neural patterns in our brain so that our behaviour is modified to be more in line with our expected goal.

There are two ways in which the mind can picture the required successful outcome. The first is in an ASSOCIATED manner and the second a DISSOCIATED manner. The manner and order in which we chose to view the outcome is very important.

Stage 1 - ASSOCIATED:

When viewing the goal outcome in this manner we are experiencing the goal as if we are physically viewing it through our own eyes. We are also experiencing the imagined senses of feelings, touch, tastes, sounds etc. as if we are physically present.

In this situation we cannot 'see' ourselves in the film-scene of the outcome's picture because we are actually imagining the experience of what it feels like to have accomplished the goal.

This is important as a first step once we have clearly identified our goal, as it gives our Unconscious mind an experience of what it would be like to have achieved the goal. This creates desire, intention and motivation within our Subconscious.

Try this exercise: Imagine yourself walking up to your dream car. Now see if you can notice your hands and your feet as you reach out and touch the hood.

Notice the colour of the car, feel the coolness of the metal under your touch. Now reach back and take the door handle and open the door. Smell that fresh new car smell as you slide yourself into the car seat and feel the comfort of it. Reach out and notice your hands closing firmly around the driving wheel. Take a firm grip. Notice how the surface feels, notice the instrument lay out.

Close the door and hear the heavy 'thunk' as the door seals out the sounds outside of the car. Now reach down and turn the car ignition. Hear that sound?

Welcome back. Did you enjoy that?

However, from a mental programming point of view it is important that we now carry out stage two.

Stage 2 - DISSOCIATED

This stage is where we pretend to jump out of our body and sit in a cinema seat to enjoy the movie of us living the goal. In this circumstance we are IN the picture, so we are actually seeing ourselves in the scene.

It is essential to do this for, if we recall that the unconscious cannot tell the difference between an imagined and real experience, if we remained viewing the goal in an associated state it would simply assume that we had accomplished our goal and therefore would not provide the energy necessary to reach the goal in real terms.

Now, imagine that you see yourself walking up to the car from the perspective of a third-party viewer. See yourself reaching out and laying your hand on the hood of the car. Now see yourself reaching back and opening the car door and sitting inside. See yourself in the car looking around and then reaching down to turn on the engine. Now imagine you driving off in your dream car, on down the road.

By seeing ourselves from outside in the film scene we are now giving the unconscious a message - "Look that's what I want, you know what it feels like to have it, wouldn't it be great to have it again?"

This is the key principle behind the use of mental rehearsal to empower goals as it helps get 'our brain in the game' and drives our motivation to succeed.

In the next chapter, I'll explain how successful advisors, coaches, mentors and leaders commit to and achieve powerful performance goals and help others to do the same.

12

Creating Practical Performance Goals

Now let's consider some of the practical work required to create effective performance goals either for ourselves or for others as a coach or mentor.

6 Keys to Success
What follows are the key steps that lead to successful goal achievement.

1. Write Down Your Goals.

The act of writing down our goals is the magic formula that externalises what up to now have been just daydreams and this simple act creates *focused* mental *intention*. It is the first act of commitment in what then becomes a process of success.

Writing down our goals creates an expectation that we can use to measure our success and to reappraise, to refocus and to recommit where necessary. It is the first action in the process of creating our successful futures. It is an absolute requirement in the science of success and determines the measure of the successes to follow as the act of writing engages our key learning modalities of sight, sound and touch and aligns the Conscious and Unconscious aspects of the mind.

2. Date Your Goals Over Ninety-Day Plus Periods.

The timing of goals is crucial. There should be enough time to allow things to occur.

As a guide goals should be scheduled over a minimum 3–6-month period (short term), 6–12-month period (medium term) or a 1–3-year period (long term). Goals *over* 3 years tend to fall into the category of life goals. They are the ideal scenarios that the short to medium term goals are creating the foundations for.

For ease of action the 12–40-week cycle is usually the most efficient for business success. This is the usual time scale I use with my coaching clients and I see powerful goals achieved in a very short time through clarity, intention, action and most importantly, accountability.

3. Review Your Goals Regularly - Repetition Makes It Work

Once written, goals need to be regularly revisited. This keeps them firmly in our minds and keeps us on the fast track to success and achievement.

It also brings in the magic of repetition. By repetition we set up new neural pathways in our minds, pathways that alter our behaviour and create new habits of success. Remember your multiplication tables... ."one by two is two, two by two is four"......a simple demonstration of the power of repetition all these years later.

4. Where Possible – Hire a Coach

Even with the best of intentions we seldom perform at our optimum when left to ourselves. Excellence is often a matter of partnership and we can benefit greatly from someone external to ourselves to hold us accountable to ourselves, someone that we can share our goals with. This could be a professional coach, a mentor or a master-mind group, a small group of selected people with whom we work with to accomplish our goals and help them to accomplish theirs.

5. Break All Large Goals Down into Sub-Goals or Actions.

Even the largest of goals can be achieved if we break them down into their smallest possible components or actions.

When broken into small and measurable actions change can then be monitored on a weekly or fortnightly basis. Actions keep you on-track towards your goals even on a daily schedule.

An 'action' can be defined as something you can do when you leave a room e.g., make a call, write a report, draft a presentation. Simple and specific.

The added advantage of breaking goals down into simple actions is that our Subconscious mind *loves* success. If we are being successful at the smaller things it provides us with more energy and *more* motivation to face the next challenge and the next and so on. Pretty soon, we've accomplished even our largest objectives.

6. Stay Flexible

Success requires flexibility.

Water travelling from a mountain spring to its ultimate goal of the sea is seldom stopped by rock. It finds a way. Over, around, under or eventually through erosion it overcomes all obstacles, refusing to contemplate failure or denial of its objective.

Setting out to create your 'future history' will create obstacles for us - after all, we have to prove we are worthy of the goal and take the learning from the process. Remember to think of the water flowing to the sea - cool, fluid and unstoppable.

The S.M.A.R.T. Model

The SMART model is a common format for structuring goals and is based on the idea of goals being drafted as follows:

S for Specific and Simple: The Unconscious mind responds to instructions that are highly specific and written in simple language.

Just as one would write a line of programming code for computer software, we keep it simple, keep it clean and keep it specific. Our goals should be simply stated and be highly specific with regards to the positive outcome we require from them.

M for Measurable and Meaningful: There has to be a means of empowering our goal success and so the goal must be of perceived value to us and so it needs to be personally meaningful enough to excite the emotions.

Only something that inspires excitement and *passion within us* can carry us forward to overcome our natural resistance to change to affect an improvement of our circumstances. This is why it is so important for a coach or mentor to assign a personal reason for the achievement of any performance goal.

A for 'As If Now' & Achievable: Goals *always* need to be expressed in the <u>present tense</u> in *order to tap the power of* our Unconscious mind.

Our Unconscious mind cannot recognise a past or a future, *only actions in the present tense* and so our goals should be stated in the present. Therefore, one of the best ways to empower goals with positive and present intent is to start with the words "I want to" or "I am".

Operational goals need to be achievable. There's little point to setting goals that are patently out of our reach. We need to have the resources necessary or can eventually access the resources necessary in time to make our goals achievable ones.

R is for Realistic & Responsible:

Goals should generally be within the bounds of our ability although this should not be an excuse for not raising our standards to improve our capabilities. For example, it would be unrealistic for most of us ordinary mortals to expect that we could survive on Mount Everest's peak in just a bathing suit.

The secret of life is this – *personal responsibility is the key to personal power.*

The more responsibility we take for our lives, career and businesses the more control we have within it. Our goals can also affect others, so we need to remember that when setting our outcomes to think in terms of consequences.

T is for Time Bound and Towards:

Set a definite deadline. When did we study the hardest for exams? (if you were a student like me then usually just the night before!). We all need a little stress to get us motivated. Without a deadline, goals are just unfulfilled dreams.

So, set a date for the goal and stick to it. Write down the day, the month and then the year. Be specific, be exact, be precise. It is a clear message to our mind that this is not negotiable, this has begun and this is when it will be done.

In the field of Neuro Linguistic Programming (NLP) there is the study of values and how they affect our beliefs. Values are emotional triggers to what attracts and repel people and they guide our behaviours.

They can have one of two directions: *Towards,* which is the positive aspect and *Away From,* which is the negative aspect.

An example of a Positive Towards goal might be 'to get rich'. If asked why, we might reply "to care for my family." That is a *'Towards'* goal as it strengthens and helps us and is motivated by care for ourselves and those close to us.

An example of a negative *'Away From'* goal might also be "to be rich" however, if asked why, we might say "so I don't want to be poor."

The need here is to move away from a negative state. While this may have short-term motivation benefits, it seldom lasts for the long-term and can create stress and encourage frustration as we find the goal harder to achieve. In fact, our performance and motivation often disappear the further away we get from the negative state we wanted to 'move away' from. It is this form of negative stress-based motivation that leads to 'boom and bust' cycles in personal motivation and performance.

Lastly, as discussed in the last chapter, all goals should have some form of mental inner representation, a picture of what it would be like to actually have the goal accomplished. This is important as a tool for programming the Unconscious and releasing the power of the mind. We often call this 'mental rehearsal' when we apply it to athletes.

The SMART goal sheet is the model to use when setting your goals for a successful future.

A good way to help identify goals would be to ask yourself the following questions:

1. What is the single *greatest* challenge facing me right now or what is the one thing I could do such that if I do it, it would affect the greatest amount of change for me

2. What sort of things would I LOVE to be doing in the job (or with my life) right now?

The first question helps us identify the most important thing that needs doing, while the second question helps us identify those things that can massively enhance our performance or our lives.

Make a list from the answers to these questions and then choose the first goal that you most want to work with. The chosen goal then requires a specific structure to be successful. It must have a **What** and a **Why** component.

The 'What' is the answer to the question *"What specifically do I want to do about this goal?"*

Then the 'Why' is the answer to the question *"why specifically is this valuable to me or what will I have that I don't have now when I make this happen?"*

These responses then allow us to structure the goal in this particular way – *"I want to ..**defined What**...so that I..**defined Why**".*

This is a well-structured and articulated goal.

Let's say that the answer to the greatest challenge is to "beat my revenue targets this year" then to define that goal into a successful goal we need to *articulate* more fully.

The first question might be: "By how much specifically, do we want to beat our revenue target?" This then sets a *specific* outcome which is clear to the conscious mind.

Let's say it is 50% (we can either write down 50% or a specific financial value) but it must be specific. This is the WHAT part of the goal and would now be written:

"I want to exceed my revenue target by 50%..."

The next part is to ensure that we find the reason WHY this of value to us. This is the *Toward* motivation or 'motive-in-action' that drives our efforts and expectations. Usually, the Why is personal and highly specific.

For example, in this goal it is easy to answer "to make more money" as the personal benefit but that is too general a reason. We need to ask "why specifically is this important to me, what will I have that I don't have at the moment when I make this goal happen" that is a powerful defining question.

From that might be *"so I can ensure my financial security"* or "so that I can take the family on holiday this year" or so that "I can create strong financial reserves" or "secure a mortgage". It is never just 'making more money', it is always highly specific and personally relevant.

Now we write in the articulated form of *"I want to exceed my revenue targets by 50% so that I create significant financial security"* – *that* is a well-defined goal.

Then underneath this articulated goal we break it into initial manageable action steps. Make as complete a list as we can and come up with as many actions as possible, the more the better.

For example, if we were going to beat our revenue target by 50%, Step 1 might be to identify three new markets for networking for prospects, Step 2 revisit previous clients, Step 3 get more active on LinkedIn for referrals and so on.

There can be more than the initial five steps (in fact many more, and the more and the simpler they are the better) but the first five or six serve to get us started on the process of making the desired outcome a range of hills rather than mountains.

Now, below these action steps write a brief description of the final thing that has to happen so that we *know* we have accomplished our goal.

In the case of this goal, it might be an image of us holding a bank statement with a large cash reserve or it might be a feeling of success in having beaten the targets or the sound of your family congratulating you on achieving the goal.

This is our *convincer.*

This is a clear signal to our Conscious and Unconscious minds that we have accomplished our target. In addition, it is also the creation of an internal visual image that assists us in harnessing our internal energies towards the achievement of our outcome.

Then set the date. When will the goal be completed? As the American motivational speaker Zig Ziglar once said "goals are just dreams with a deadline". If there is no specific date attached to the goal then all our careful planning is wasted.

Dates can be 3, 6 and 9 months away or even more depending on the size of the goal. What is most important is that we set a day, a month and the year as this focuses the mind wonderfully on a specific deadline for completion.

The Action Plan

From this initial goal setting exercise we might set two or three goals.

If so then we might want to create an Action Plan, something that allows us to choose selected actions from several goals so that we can focus on moving forward on all our goals at the same time, by focusing only on taking the actions that we assign to a given week.

Used weekly, the action plan continues the process of breaking our goals into bite-size chunks that we can easily accomplish on a day-to-day, week-to-week basis. This then ensures that we get closer and closer to our successful outcomes.

The sheet is simple to create.

Take another piece of paper and write down (specifically and simply) up to five or six *accomplishable* things (selected from all of our chosen goals) that can be done in a given week or fortnight that will bring you towards your outcome or outcomes.

Make sure that these things are in your ownership i.e., that you are not depending on someone else to make it happen. Control what you control directly, *influence* through others what you cannot control and everything else is something we simply 'accept for now', as we can't do anything about it.

From the actions that we complete, new actions will then present themselves. The dynamic that comes from taking action presents new challenges and opportunities that we can address to accomplish our desired goal.

To do so effectively, *prioritise* the new actions required on the action plan and complete them. For even greater success not only *deadline the action plan* but *micro-deadline the actions* stating when in the week each action will itself be completed.

For this it can be excellent to have a professional coach to be your performance partner holding you accountable to yourself to deliver on the action plans and the goals.

Having someone who holds us accountable to ourselves, knowing that on a certain day, at a certain time, we have to sit down with someone and account for what we have or have not done is a powerful tool for keeping us on track and moving towards success.

Success follows along with a greater sense of self-esteem and confidence in our abilities to create the world in our own unique way.

Successful professionals know that their lives and careers move from 'mediocre to magnificent' and from 'success to significance', when we engage with effective goal setting and coaching.

13

Managing Your Professional Time

Busy professionals can be constantly time challenged. The question is… are they being efficient or effective? Efficient means that you are doing the job *right*. Effective means that are you doing the *right* job.

I find that a huge amount of professional time is wasted by our focusing on the wrong things. Working with my many coaching clients they consistently raise the issue of 'time management' as being a recurring challenge and as a result how they cope with their rapidly changing environments, work and home demands.

I recall my old mentor and friend the wonderful speaker, author and behavioural psychologist Dr. Denis Waitley once said that "Time management is a fallacy, you can't manage time. One cannot make an hour longer than it is or bring yesterday back to today".

He said that it is our *focus* that we should manage and not our time. Manage your focus and time starts to work for you.

Would it not be fair to say that as experts, leaders, executives, managers, sales professionals, relationship managers, professional advisers and consultants (where time and expertise are often our only resources) we often get too absorbed into the business and lose our sense of what also matters in life?

As a result we may find ourselves wishing there were 24 hours in the working day. We may find that we are reacting and fire-fighting rather than being proactive and in control, with not enough time for the important things like self and family.

If you'd like to get more control over your time or your personal organisation and make more time to strategize, advise or spend time doing the important things in life then here are a few ideas on how to get back on top on your time:

1 .Schedule 'Virtual' Meetings.

Ask yourself this question, who is your *most* important client or internal stakeholder? If they wanted to meet with you right now you'd meet them, wouldn't you? You'd drop everything to be there for them now right?

But how about reflecting on the fact that YOU are your most important client?

How about planning a regular weekly 'client' meeting with yourself, with your 'virtual self' sitting opposite you at the table and wanting to know where things are and what you need to do to get the most out of things? What if you were the CEO of your own business. What reflective time are you allocating to all the elements of what makes your 'service business' i.e. the services you contract into your role. Or what time are you setting aside for self-reflection or proactive planning? Do you want to create the future or just hope it works out?

Create a time in the diary every week when you have a one hour meeting with yourself. Draft a written agenda for what you want to 'discuss' with yourself or reflect on and this is one meeting that NEVER gets de-prioritised or re-scheduled. Do this during office hours and either do it your office, a meeting room or go offsite to a coffee shop where you write. Make sure you have that meeting without interruption from others.

Every one of us can benefit from the ability to create some enforced reflective space. But unless we diarise it and treat it like an important client meeting, it never happens. Without investing in ourselves, pretty soon we run out of the energy to invest in others – and in our business and our career, that's crucial.

2. Delegate!

Every leader and manager worth their pay grade should be able to delegate effectively yet few know how to manage it. So here are some suggestions that will help.

First, make a list of what exactly you do. Everything.

Then think about what each hour of 'routine stuff' that you can hand to someone else can earn you if you are working on the 'money stuff'. Prioritise what you decide to keep and what you want to 'hand off'.

Second, make a list of the talents of your team members, associates, colleagues or sales support.

What are their strengths? What are their career goals? How can you help them grow skills or provide a reward or help build their profile by allocating a relevant project or task to them? Let them show you what they can do for you and always delegate to their strengths.

Don't just give them the rubbish stuff either. Hand over things that will challenge them and help them grow or that gives them some 'face time' with (and recognition from) more senior stakeholders. There should be some obvious benefit in doing it for them.

Third, involve them in the solution of how best to handle the matter.

Discuss with them what exactly you want and invite their views on how they can make it happen. It doesn't always have to be your way. That which we co-create, we own. The more they input into how they will handle it, the more likely they are to take ownership and responsibility for it and so deliver in it.

Lastly, agree to check back with them at regular intervals and then let them get on with it.

3. Make Personal Time.

Why do you do what you do? Taking time out for you is the best way to recharge and it is something many of us fail to do.

Years from now it won't be the late nights at the office that we will fondly remember but the moments and memories with family and friends that forge the life we want to reflect fondly on. Family and friends may respect what we do but it's us they love and want with them not our work. Since Covid-19 and with more of us working at home the management of personal and work boundaries has become even more challenging with many of us suffering from 'boundary creep'. We need to decide on and rigidly enforce the boundaries between our personal and professional worlds.

Surveys have shown that the most successful professionals routinely plan the vacations they intend to take at the start of each year. Knowing they are taking regular breaks helps them to stay motivated for a specific, intense period of time. Then they go, get rested and come back with even greater energy.

Even weekly personal time can be beneficial and all it takes is a decision to make it happen.

Try this experiment. Head home or wrap up in your home office, one day a week, every week, for the next three weeks at 4pm or 3pm – no later, pick a time. Start as early as you like but lead the traffic home once a week or step away from the desk and plan something with family and friends.

I notice 'boundary creep' particularly with people working with global companies and from home that still look to run industrial age 9-5pm schedules in a digital and hybrid world where they have colleagues working 24/7. They end up taking calls at 11pm at night. Now you might say that's the job, fine, no issue with that. But if this is regular thing don't imagine you will work from 9-5pm and then do the calls. Adapt your schedule accordingly. Start later. Change your schedule. Adapt and thrive.

You may find what a previous client of mine once found, that the extra hours he was putting in had become a habit but one that was neither necessary nor productive. Work expands to fill every vacuum.

4. Manage Your Focus and Your Professional Boundaries.

It's tempting to chase all the business there is, to go from contract to contract, deal to deal, project to project especially if we're always focused on the money or the promotion. It's tempting to say 'we can do it' to every request that comes from clients or even colleagues particularly senior ones.

The problem is that we quickly find that we are being very busy but not every effective. Then we blame poor 'time management' as the problem when actually what we are doing is letting our professional boundaries 'creep'.

The real challenge is managing our focus, *what* we really should be doing and *why* we really should be doing it. It's a bit like business meetings. How many business meetings do you attend that really are a waste of time?

Try using this filter for the future:

*1. **Must See or Must Do:*** Is this a person that I really need to be there for? (a client or senior stakeholder) Is this project something I really need to do?

*2. **Nice to See or Nice to Do:*** If you do the Must and have time remaining then this is where you invest it. With people who can help build your profile or career, investing in people that can get things done for you when you need it, your networks or the projects and plans that can help add value or interest to your role and help you stand out from the norm.

*3. **Deferrable/Delegate-able:*** This is for both people and activities and see how you win back more time for the important things. If they're not a "Must Do" or not a "Nice to Do" then it or they can be delegated or deferred.

Learn to push back by saying "No" elegantly or say "No, for now". Do not simply accept things because they are put in front of you. Push back a little, challenge their perceived need and balance it against your resources to deliver.

Ask people:

"Does this need to be done now?" OR

"I am busy right now but I could get to it tomorrow would that be OK?" OR

"X is the real expert in this area you really should reach out to them..."

Just because people ask doesn't mean we always have to automatically or immediately take something on board. The last person you want to be seen as is someone who over-promises and under-delivers OR someone so important, so important to the running of your team that you can never be promoted out of that role.

5 . The CIA Formula

Effectiveness comes down to levels of control. I developed an additional tool that I call the CIA filter or formula (that I drafted from The Serenity Prayer) to help clients cope with managing focus and is a great little tool for self-awareness of the limits of our control.

First, make a list of all the things that you think you need to get done or actions that you have to do. Then apply the following filter/formula to the list:

C = Control or Act on What You Own (First Level of Control)

Note the things that you directly have authority for or control over and make happen without reference to anyone else. Do these first.

I = Influence or Reach Out to Others (Second Level of Control)

This is about leverage and the quality of your professional relationships and is where your internal and external networks become important.

So, for things we don't directly control or can act on, we need *to reach out and influence someone else* who has the power to make sure that an action comes to pass.

So 'I or Influence' is therefore any goal or task that requires us to influence someone else to do it for us, takes a little longer to happen and we have less control over the outcome.

A = Accept for Now (Third Level of Control)

This is another level of self-control and self-respect.

I see too many professionals beating themselves up over things that they do not control and cannot influence even though there is really nothing that they can do here. Just becoming aware of that and focusing on what you can directly control or have others influence for you makes us far more effective and happier.

We need to leave that which we have no control or influence over alone. In time it may become a 'C' or an 'I' but most likely it will just fade away because it was never important in the first place.

Remember while our work is important both to ourselves and our clients, we work to live not live to work.

Take just some of these steps and watch your energy rise and realise something, your professional productivity increases when you take adequate personal time to recharge and you take back control.

14

Steps to Being an Influencer in the New Digital World

The Covid-19 crisis brought about the single biggest change in working practice in a hundred years. With it, the world suddenly and unexpectedly accelerated almost entirely into the digital realm. This presented real challenges for modern leaders, executives and sales professionals, not least of which being how to reach out to build trust at a distance to create new business relationships or influence and manage their clients and teams remotely.

There is a further element to this in that the crisis has also accelerated the adoption of AI (or artificial intelligence) in the workplace. AI is already replacing transactional work, sales and management practices and can carry out the monitoring of staff performance remotely now that everybody is more tied to a screen in our new hybrid and remote professional world.

What it cannot replace (at least not yet) is the need for leaders, executives and sales professionals who can build empathy and trust with others, inspire performance, motivation, creativity, synergy and success. People who don't just lead from a position of expertise but from a position of influence and service. People who act as highly trusted and influential advisors, coaches and mentors.

To put it simply, to succeed in this digital and increasingly AI-enabled world then sales professionals, executive and leaders need to be strategic, creative and relational and not transactional and therefore replaceable.

In this last chapter I want to cover some simple tips and ideas about how better to project your brand and presence in the digital world. How to approach meetings, how to run meetings and how to follow-up on meetings to ensure that executives and sales professionals can build and maintain an effective personal brand or executive presence and high levels of trust with their clients and key stakeholders in the new digital world of AI.

<u>Before a Meeting:</u>

1 . Create a LinkedIn profile, ask for recommendations and connect on LinkedIn in advance

LinkedIn is the largest professional social network in the world, period. If you're not on it you need to be. Here's why. Trust in a world where social distancing and isolation is the norm means that trust is now built entirely online. If you do not have a professional profile on LinkedIn it means you don't exist in the new digital world.

When professionals look to build a new relationship with a contact, or if we receive a communication from someone we do not already know, our default action is now to check out their profile on LI.

What conclusion would you say people make about us when they:

1. They can't find any profile of us on LI
2. We have an incomplete profile
3. We have no connections on our profile
4. We have no photograph on our profile or a personal photo rather than a business photo or
5. We have few or no recommendations or testimonials on our profile?

How likely is it that they are making judgements about who we are as a person right now and they're probably not positive judgements that help to build trust, gain attention and get a relationship off to a good start.

At the time of writing LinkedIn is a critical tool for modern business and we need to be able to use the platform (or any social media platform that evolves as the 'go to' business social network in the future) to reinforce existing relationships, share company news, run events, connect with new contacts and especially connect with those contacts before or after a digital or virtual meeting as a means of creating a platform to deepen a relationship.

2 . Build a 'Credibility Bank'

A 'credibility bank' is something a leader, executive or sales professional should work to build when they wish to demonstrate their expertise and further enhance trust online.

Having a LinkedIn profile can also help with this, or we might do this on our internal company intranet or Slack channel. For example, on our profile we can post or share articles, reports, videos and podcasts that might be of interest to our contacts (think team members, colleagues, clients and stakeholders). We can 'Like' or ideally comment on posts created or shared by these same connections, indicating to them that we are engaging with their interests and listening to their online voices.

In addition, we should consider presenting at any of the numerous webinars and digital events that may be happening within our firm or offer to be a host or a member of an expert panel for our client firms, industry or professional associations. If we're not comfortable presenting then perhaps offer to host or facilitate a breakout or discussion room at the virtual conference or event.

Better yet, it's easier than ever to organise our own where we control the guest list.

Any of the above activities can help to raise your brand, extend your executive presence, build trust and influence through demonstrating your expertise and in the new digital world where people do not have a chance to interact personally, seeing a person's expertise demonstrated is both reassuring and builds confidence.

3 . Use Google Alerts

In advance of a digital meeting or event first research the prospect, client, company or individual stakeholder on LinkedIn and then set up a Google Alert on them or their business.

Setting up a Google Alert on a person or company means that we get an alert or notification every time something new about them shows up on the internet. Forewarned is forearmed.

This is a very effective and simple way to receive up-to-date information on individuals or companies as articles, videos and website updates once shared on the internet are brought to our attention immediately.

<u>During a Digital or Online Meeting:</u>

1 . Be Personable

The digital world is a less formal world than the office so when we speak in this medium think 'conversation rather than presentation'.

Remove a lot of the formality of presentations and focus instead on having a conversation. Minimise the length of our slide decks, make sure we focus on the camera on the laptop (positioned at eye level with the right lighting and backdrop) and not on the image on the screen.

Presenting and engaging in the digital world is more like TV presenting than live presenting and looking at the camera gives the other person the perspective that we are looking directly at and addressing them. Looking at their image rather than the camera lens however means that our eye contact appears poor and poor eye contact never helps with building rapport and trust.

Try to speak at a medium pace as this is more suited to a digital presentation and be aware of our dress and appearance. Dress is more relaxed in the digital world but should always be smart business casual (at least from the waist up!) and if we are in a meeting keep our camera on. It sends a poor message around our level of engagement in a meeting if people cannot get any feedback because we're not on screen.

2 . Be a Master of Questions and Suggestions

To build trust with someone always start by encouraging other people to do the talking. Allow a short pause when they finish speaking to ensure that they have indeed finished and it's not just a lag on the line. Also learn to become more comfortable with asking questions and suggesting ideas rather than directing the conversation.

Encourage others to speak, to volunteer ideas, to make suggestions to solve problems. Ask them to clarify and specify their responses so there is no confusion between all the parties.

Get comfortable with facilitating rather than directing conversations, people will value a person who is seen to support and serve rather than command in this new world. The new definition of leadership is to create the environment in which others can excel. In this new world of remote working teams this is especially true.

Facilitate, make suggestions rather than statements and try to avoid arguments. Trust is hard to build in the digital space and easy to lose. Be an advisor rather than a 'seller' or 'director'.

3 . Show Your Hands, Look at the Camera and Actively Listen.

Operating in the digital world is operating in a 2D world and not a 3D world. Much of what we unconsciously pick up when we are assessing people and making a decision about whether we trust them or not is absent in a 2D world. Our 'Spidey senses' don't work so well when we're on Zoom or MS Teams.

Therefore to build the level of trust that comes before influence there are some simple things that we can do. The first is as I've already mentioned look at the camera lens and not the image. This gives the impression that we are addressing the person directly and making good eye contact. Good eye contact is essential to building trust and appearing sincere to others.

Secondly, when we're speaking be a little more animated in our gestures and show our hands. When people can see our hands on screen it helps to build rapport. Being overly formal and stiff can sometimes create resistance from or discomfort in others.

Lastly, Paraphrase ("let me just see if I understand what you're saying"), Summarise ("so what we've on agreed is") and use simple language that matches the language that the other person is using. This clearly demonstrates to the other person that we are actively listening and engaged in the meeting and are fully present. This keeps the other person's attention focused on you, allowing you to exert more influence in the meeting.

Here's a quick check list of things to also be aware of online:

- Look relaxed and calm
- Look into the camera not at the person
- Dress appropriately (smart casual or more serious dress – match the participants)
- Have a professional background (avoid green screen if possible and arrange your surroundings to be interesting but not distracting)
- Project with energy (need to project more energy when presenting to a screen)
- Consider standing up (if you are presenting)
- Avoid distractions

- Have the right lighting (check your face is not in shadow or lighting too strong)
- Have your sound right (Unmute!)

After a Meeting:

1 . Follow-up immediately

After any digital meeting, follow-up immediately. Out of sight is out of mind in the digital world so make sure that you deliver what you promised as close to the call or virtual meeting as possible to remain relevant.

If it's a report or documents, then maybe offer a follow-up virtual call where you can 'walk them through' the data.

2 . Create a contact strategy

As well as following-up immediately, to build presence and influence in the digital world retaining the attention of a client or stakeholder is critical. Staying 'front of mind' so that they are thinking of us when it comes to their needs is crucial. Today, 'share of attention equals share of influence'.

To help with this it is useful to create a 'contact strategy' or a strategy that ensures that the person we are looking to influence receives some communication of value from us on a regular basis. An email with a relevant report attached, an introduction to someone of value to them, a gift of a book, a link to an industry or company report or an invite to a 'virtual' coffee.

It's worth defining listing our key stakeholders, identifying the areas of most value to them and then creating a proactive contact strategy to ensure that our 'brand' with clients and stakeholders remains strong.

Hopefully, some of the above tips will help when it comes to creating and maintaining trust and influence while leading teams and winning and retaining high value clients in this new digital world.

To remain successful and to thrive in this new hybrid and digital world it is important that experts, executives and professionals learn that our expertise is no longer the currency that matters in the new digital world of AI but the ability to build trust and connect, to understand and be able to successfully influence our key stakeholders, our teams and our clients.

About the Author

Sean is an international G2S® and Marshal Goldsmith certified leadership coach, conference speaker and sales and communications trainer with expertise in influential leadership and sales communications, driving team and individual performance and creating winning pitches and speeches. He is also the founder of the G2S Executive Coaching School, a CPD certified program for training high performance leaders and consultants as executive coaches.

Sean is an engineer by profession who can take complex concepts in leadership, sales, communications and coaching and create highly practical tool kits for his clients to help them excel in all areas.

Sean is the author of three books; 'Invoking the Feminine: Strength, Love and Wisdom' (2019) 'C.A.S.H: Coaching As a Side Hustle' (2020) and 'The Highly Trusted Advisor: How to Win Clients and Lead Teams in the Hybrid Age' (2021) plus several e-books on management and sales communications.

His interests include martial arts, fitness, horse riding, film and photography, historical fiction, travel and a glass or three of nice wine. He lives in Dublin, Ireland with his wife Sharon, their two sons Nicholas and Gregory and their dog Kai.

You can reach him and share your thoughts on the book with him at sean@seanweafer.com

Printed in Great Britain
by Amazon

66906714R00097